Elusive Quest for Freedom

Elusive Quest for Freedom

The Healing BALM

Published by Huaca Enterprises

Copyright © 2010 by The Healing Balm

Published by
Huaca Enterprises LLC.
P.O. Box 110003
Atlanta, Ga. 30311

All rights reserved. No part of this publication may be reproduced, stored in a retrieval system or transmitted, in any form, or by any means, electronic, mechanical, recorded, photocopied, or otherwise, without the prior permission of the copyright owner, except by a reviewer who may quote brief passages in a review.

Printed in the United States of America

ISBN: 978-0-578-05584-8

Contents

Acknowledgments 7
Introduction 9

Part 1: Loss of Identity 13
    Chapter 1: Foreign Invasion 15
    Chapter 2: Re-thinking Slavery and Freedom 23
    Chapter 3: Behavior of a Virus 29
    Chapter 4: To Steal, Kill and Destroy 39
    Chapter 5: Defining the Box 51
    Chapter 6: Prisoners of War 59
    Chapter 7: Name It and Claim It 65
    Chapter 8: Four Steps of the Immune System 69

Part 2: Incomplete Identity 73
    Chapter 9: Afrocentrism 75
    Chapter 10: Pan-Africanism and Other Connections 85
    Chapter 11: Origin of blacks in the Americas 95
    Chapter 12: Mother Earth, America and Africa 105
    Chapter 13: Oral Traditions 111
    Chapter 14: Liberating Identity 121

Part 3: Restoring Identity 133
    Chapter 15: Liberation Theology 135
    Chapter 16: Feminine Descriptions of God 153
    Chapter 17: Androgynous Descriptions of God 165

Part 4: Epilogue 173
    Chapter 18: Invasion and Healing 175
    Chapter 19: A Nation Standing 181
    Chapter 20: Liberation Game 199

    Notes 203
    References 205

Acknowledgments

I would like to give a special thanks to Antonio Pacheco for showing me how to critically analyze religious scripture back in the late 1980s. The technique and insight I learned from him has been extended to other literature, sermons and ideas in general. The next decade was spent mainly learning from the guidance of Dr. William White. He shaped my critical analysis and brought it into a Native American sphere of understanding. Pearson Cotton, Victor Trimble and Antonio Winston shared in the travels, dialogue and research that are the foundation for this work. I started putting my thoughts together in poetic form as I interpreted our research. An English PhD candidate in Atlanta showed me how to structure poetic flows, but unfortunately, I cannot recall her name to properly acknowledge her. Originally, I wrote a book of poetry to reflect a view of the world that has been only narrowly applied to the very small population of so-called red people. After several literary discussions with my Mother, it was determined that books of poetry are not taken seriously.

At the behest of Vince Rogers and others, I set out to put Dr. White's teaching into a coherent body of information that could be easily shared with others. Still I felt it was missing a necessary spiritual component. Toward including this information, Chris Burnett and Ayanna Thompson set up small meetings that enabled us to develop the spiritual concepts of survival and sustainability relevant to our experience in the U.S. After nine months of dialogue, we began to approach the story again using prose rather than poetry. Upon completing the basic manuscript, Dr. Mack Jones reviewed it and provided comments that have greatly improved and polished the finished version of this book. My own Father has been supportive of this work even though he may not agree with the spiritual implications. Tina Benton, Venus Prather and Janice Sears have been especially supportive in discussing solutions to oppression on an almost daily basis. It is inevitable that some contributors will be left out. Please accept my general acknowledgment of all those who contributed to making this information available.

Introduction

It has been said that when an elder dies, a library of information perishes as well. The primary motivation for this book is the loss of information from Dr. William White. He did not write any books that we are aware of, so we put the first two sections of this information together from his teachings. We are going to discuss foreign invasion in a liberating manner, not in an apologetic manner. We have been tip toeing around freedom for the last 40 years. This has allowed Black Americans in the U.S. to slip into a worse situation than was prevalent in the 1960s. Freedom movements were crushed mercilessly by the same government that we are supposed to trust. Our solidarity has been dismantled. Our desire to be free has been almost extinguished. This is what scares us the most. As we enter challenging times of global crises and change, Black Americans have become like pets who do not even want to be free. The context for our struggle is not only genocidal aggression, but also acceptance of this genocide. If love is to conquer hate, then this love must encompass defense from the aggression of the State and its cohorts. We do not have to return murder with murder, but we can create disincentives for them to stop the aggression, thereby creating a peaceful place for our children to survive and thrive.

In the first section of the book, we redefine the racial antagonism between the invader and the invaded. This relationship can only be healed to yield equality as each group controls its own space and destiny. We frame our argument as a relationship between an invading virus and a body that must heal itself to survive. This is going to be uncomfortable for some readers. We respect this, so be advised that this is not a comfort book. Excessive creature comforts are actually a large part of the problem. Our insulated comfort enables us to turn a blind eye to the constant invasions against people from the global south. People are murdered typically because of a misunderstanding about relationships. We hurt each other because we do not understand our relationship to each other. Likewise, we hurt Mother Earth because we do not understand our relationship to her. For example, people don't rape their mothers. But when we frame our relationship with our Mother as an object to be exploited, like a prostitute, then rape and abuse becomes acceptable, even normalized. In an effort to heal the wounds of this self-destruction, we conclude our first section with a discussion of the immune system.

So, this book is largely about political, physical and spiritual relationships. There is an undeniable adversarial relationship between the dominating culture in the U.S. and others who have been color coded as red, brown and black. The invaders from the north, who brought us the blues, came from many different European countries. The victims of invasion with respect to the development of the U.S. are from many different countries of the Southern Atlantic. The result for Black Americans in particular is an acute identity crisis. In the second section of this book, we contribute to an alternative view of our origins and identity in the U.S. It has become clear that black people were here long before Columbus. We offer additional insight about who we are. We cannot even begin to become players in the international game of survival if we do not understand who we are individually and as a nation. One problem with Pan-Africanism as a political position and physical identity is that we must first have an identity of our own rather than existing only within a larger parent group. This actually demonstrates a continued subordinated mentality. We talk against self-hate, but we practice it every day because we have not overcome our crisis of identity. In solution, we reconnect with an indigenous identity such that our survival in the Americas as a sovereign people is attainable and sustainable.

In part three of the book, we take an understanding of our relationships to an almost metaphysical level. This enables us to expand beyond Western European intellectual limitations into power that can be used to finally overcome domination. Again we frame things differently in this section. We cannot reach an adequate understanding of who we are through Western European schooling (including African American Studies) and Middle Eastern religion. Both are misleading. As we begin to see the light, we will learn to use our moments of solitude to expand our power through meditation rather than filling our time with computers and video games. We have to remember that our ancestry is both external and internal. The internal part is off limits to the invader. For this reason, he bombards us with entertainment so that we will not develop our sense of self that is off limits to him. In order to overcome historical oppression in particular, we will have to develop that part of our historical consciousness that the aggressor cannot invade and cannot control. Knowledge of our Atlantic and Southeastern U.S. identity strengthens our connection with each other and with the land on which we need to survive.

As we tread on spiritual ground, we remain connected to reality through a practical, philosophical and theoretical understanding of Nature. We use the tools of ancestral teachings, logic and science to build a bridge between people who are religious, metaphysical or anti-religious. We do this by explaining our spiritual origins using the Virgin Mother story that we are all familiar with. It is a starting point for developing improved framework of liberation theology. Having a spiritual foundation is very important, because then we retain an understanding of what is going on even when the invading virus mutates or changes the meaning or the names of his aggression. Without spiritual development, we are less than the beasts of the field. This is evidenced by our level of self-destruction as opposed to that of other animals. Perennial spiritual grounding will help make us less vulnerable to manipulation. The solution that will heal Black America is no different from the solution that will heal the Earth, which is no different from the solution that will heal other oppressed people. It comes from a better way of defining and understanding relationships.

In the epilogue, we summarize the process of invasion and healing. We want to make it clear that we cannot heal the wounds of dysfunction with a Republican form of governance. This makes it too easy for us to be sold out by a few corruptible leaders. We can learn from the mistakes of many African countries and from some of the successes of countries like Cuba and Venezuela. We can develop our organizations such that every 2,000 people or so are adequately represented. Obviously, we have to ensure that there are poor people sitting in the leadership meetings. This is one of the main differences between a Republic and a participatory Democracy. Wealthy people have not proven to make good decisions for poor people. The poor are no less capable of governing themselves than wealthy people are. One requirement is that access to education without debt has to be ensured. Our mixed income leaders must also recognize our human right to land on which to survive. Land reforms are an essential part of liberation. Every family must have land and be taught how to use it sustainably. We conclude in the epilogue with a discussion of invasion and healing followed by an acronym that helps put it all together and a game that can be used for accountability.

Enjoy the reading on your journey through the Elusive Quest for Freedom. Let the healing begin.

PART 1

LOSS OF IDENTITY

"In order to oppress any organism, one must create an identity crisis."
Dr. William White

Chapter 1

Foreign Invasion

THE foreign invasion of North America and the subsequent foreign invasions from the U.S. are destroying our entire planet and future in unbridled aggression towards 90% of the rest of the world's population. As we approach the second decade of the new millennium, the U.S. is fast becoming the source of everybody's anger. Well, when people are invaded and murdered and robbed, they get angry. The victims are forced to operate with infected mental, emotional and social wounds. As memories were destroyed with the invasion of the Southeastern U.S. in particular, the perspectives and embellishments of the foreigner have become compulsory history. Buried under the rubble of lost land, loved ones and memories, at least one group has lost its identity. Black Americans have been crippled with an oppressive identity crisis. As quoted at the beginning of this section, Dr. White taught that in order to oppress any organism, one has to create and maintain an identity crisis. This is the essential problem this book aims to solve, the open wound that has to be healed. The survivability of any species is directly related to its knowledge of the whole self. The reasoning in this first section is to explain from a different perspective what has caused our loss of identity.

The identity crisis can be categorized as a spiritual, political, economic, psychological, social or cultural problem. However the crisis is disguised, it will predictably lead to genocide if we do not change our direction from symptomatic treatments to cures. Most of our recent struggles are only treating the symptoms of our problems while we become increasingly more entrenched into the same unhealthy and oppressive system. The fight for sovereignty until the 1960's is becoming erased from our memories and mention as we dig more deeply into the grave state of a permanent underclass. The teaching of Dr. William White and the remaining content of this book become necessary because our current leaders and the current approaches to liberation do not provide a lasting cure for our crisis of identity.

We have been building on the teachings of Dr. White since his transition. We will add some spiritual elements to his historical and cultural teachings. Like the Hebrews writing of liberation from Egypt, we are going to include lessons from liberation theology. In terms of how this relates to our identity, we will bring out important insights about our spiritual heritage. In an effort to explain this thoroughly, we will go all the way back to our cosmic beginning. We will not start here and follow a chronological path, however. We just wanted to point out that, although we may start in the middle of the story, we will not leave out the beginning. We will share information on this when we get to the religious part of our identity crisis. We will explain why the bishop was put on the chess board and how capturing the soul of the people is an integral part of an offensive strategy to win the war of domination. It weakens the resolve of the victims and makes them easier to defeat and enslave.

When we discuss the bishop in the war game, we are not referring to just the catholic order. We are referring to the religious men or women in general who are given the task of capturing souls for the invading polity. Unfortunately, we know that in many cases when the victims could not be converted, they were mercilessly tortured and killed often by the clergy of the invading religious order who claimed to bring salvation to the people. We know, for example, that there were religious men who came with Columbus, although not on his first trip. Since the essential problem of our identity is a result of European invasion of the Americas, we will start off here with explaining the causes of our identity crisis. In other words, this is yet another manuscript on knowledge of self. What makes this writing different is that the focus is on the Indigenous self rather than the African self. From this view of the world, we can better develop a mind set and strategy that liberates us from European domination.

In this text, we establish a different view of who we are and who we are not. We know that we are not the dominator. We are the dominated. We are not the invader. We are the invaded. We are not the aggressive predator. We are being penalized for being civilized. Unlike Black American people, hyper aggressive Europeans have developed the idea that they have a divine right to rule the world. Whether it is genes or memes or some other force unseen, we can be sure that it is played out as domination over all other people, indeed over all other life forms. Hebrew and Christian religious scripture has contributed significantly to licensing the European superiority complex from which they interpret a divine right to rule the world. The Hebrew scribes wrote of man's dominion in the first chapter of the first book of their holy scripture. The King James Version of the Bible reads, "…have dominion over the fish of the sea and over the fowl of the air, and over every living thing that moveth upon the earth."[1] We will cover more on this later. We just wanted to set up the context of thinking that Europeans brought with them as they invaded the Americas beginning in 1492.

As Jan Carew put it, "For centuries, we have been fed on an intellectual diet of the glories of that period while its crimes, its monstrous medieval cruelties, its racism and the genocidal holocausts it unleashed have been ignored."[2] The monstrous medieval cruelties that Jan Carew wrote about are not only medieval. This is the monstrous nature of the European that surfaces any time he does not get what he wants. In other words, any time there is resistance to his domination. This monstrous behavior is not an isolated mistake that occurred in the distant past, such as only in the medieval period or only when Europeans invaded the Americas. While Manifest Destiny is undeniably the worst human holocaust the world has ever known, historical and contemporary times are replete with examples of this behavior. Neocolonialism and globalization are the new buzz words for this aggression that is still assumed to be sanctioned by God.

For example, in 2005 Pat Robertson, a well known televangelist, spoke openly about the assassination of President Hugo Chavez. There are countless examples of this behavior but we will just cite a few from different periods. In Frederick Douglas' Fourth of July speech in 1852, he spoke of Europeans in the U.S. as guilty of the most shocking and bloody violence in the world. The following is the last paragraph from his speech:

> "Go search where you will, roam through all the monarchies and despotisms of the Old World, travel through South America, search out every abuse and when you have found the last, lay your facts by the side of the everyday practices of this nation, and you will say with me that, for revolting barbarity and shameless hypocrisy, America reigns without rival."[3]
>
> Frederick Douglas

In the post-slavery environment, the violence against America's people of color had not diminished. In 1918, Claude McKay wrote of the same monstrous behavior that Jan Carew described as medieval and Frederick Douglas described as barbaric. We have included one of his poems entitled, *If We Must Die*:

> "If we must die, let it not be like hogs
> Hunted and penned in an inglorious spot,
> While round us bark the mad and hungry dogs,
> Making their mock at our accursed lot.
> If we must die, O let us nobly die,
> So that our precious blood may not be shed
> In vain; then even the monsters we defy
> Shall be constrained to honor us though dead!
> O kinsmen! we must meet the common foe!
> Though far outnumbered let us show us brave,
> And for their thousand blows deal one deathblow!
> What though before us lies the open grave?
> Like men we'll face the murderous, cowardly pack
> Pressed to the wall, dying, but fighting back!"[4]
>
> Claude McKay

This is well after the so-called slavery period, yet we find the same cruelties to be consistent through time. In 1967, Martin Luther King Jr. (M.L.K.) spoke of Europeans in the U.S. as the greatest purveyors of violence in the world in his stance against the war in Vietnam. And in 2008, Europeans in the U.S. admitted to the same monstrous cruelties in Iraq that have been practiced at least since the medieval period in Europe. This chronology makes it clear that we are not dominated by a creature that has changed his ways. In spite of all of this, the invader has the unmitigated gall to try to teach our children that we are the same as him. It is no wonder that we have an extreme identity crisis.

The essential problem with the idea of sameness is that it takes away our ability to understand who we are. We learn that we are essentially dark skinned white people, particularly when we take in the linear teaching that everyone comes from Africa. We will cover this issue in more detail later.

For now, we are discussing a serious problem with the identity crisis that cripples our ability to understand ourselves and consequently our ability to defend from non-self. An immune system analogy is instructive here. All of our cells have cell markers which identify who we are. When foreign invading material enters our bodies, our immune system goes to work to remove this foreign material from our systems. If our bodies cannot recognize that which is foreign, then our defense system is rendered ineffective and we will perish. We will die from foreign invasion. This describes the state of Black American identity. We are no longer able to recognize that which is foreign, which leaves us on a genocidal track. We have an ethno-cultural disease similar to AIDS.

We will cover solutions to this problem. First let's continue to look at the causes. We are suggesting so far that the cause of our identity crisis is foreign invasion and a subsequent weakening of our immune (cultural defense) system. We must thoroughly understand the causes of this problem in order to develop a strategy that will keep this from ever happening again. At this point we cannot say, 'Never Again.' Europeans in the U.S. can put us back into chattel slavery any time they get ready because we are unprepared to defend ourselves. They actually never stopped this activity with the legal slavery of prisons. Our powerlessness is not derived from our lack of weaponry. Our impotence derives from not having a clear view of our identity which is the foundation of our unity. We cannot defend ourselves from foreign invasion because we do not know what is foreign. We are going to share some things about Europeans to help us learn what is foreign. It may come across as an angry diatribe. It may be viewed as polemic. We cannot be deterred by this, however, because we are headed for genocide. In this book, you will find the honest, angry and painful language that reflects the reality of our situation. We will not deprecate agitation. The situation of continued subjugation and inhumane treatment, like ramming screwdrivers and night sticks up our behinds, is deplorable and reprehensible. To paraphrase further from Douglas' speech, we will not equivocate. We will not apologize. We will use the severest language we can command. Our immune systems are not apologetic about foreign invasion. We endeavor to discover the truth about who we are in an effort to bring about a healthier balance of leadership for ourselves and the world.

The purpose of this section of the book is to give us a clear picture of

European invasion from the perspective of the victim so that we will never let him invade us again. We have to join with the forces that disallow his continued destruction of Mother Earth and her children. This is not concerned with whether we have some nice European friends in the U.S. whom we may upset. This is about whether we want to survive or not. The causes of the problem with our identity are the same as the causes of the destruction of Mother Earth. This brings us back to the European invasion of the Americas and the mentality that they came here with. We have already mentioned the mindset of a divine right to rule the world. Let us add in that this divinity was built on an avaricious and religious ego, not on the divinity of Mother Nature. The Eurocentric rule of law was born out of an intransigent desire to dominate the world. It was not born out of the laws of Nature. European's refusal to heed to the laws of Nature is causing the entire system that supports human life to be destroyed.

It is our firm conviction that Black Americans may be the only people who can stop the self-fulfilling prophecy of inevitable destruction. The illusions of power in charge are well aware of this. It is no mystery as to why J. Edgar Hoover stated that the Black Panther Party was the greatest threat to the internal security of the U.S. The rise of Black America would set off a chain of cascading events that would completely de-rail European dominance all over the world. When the identity of Black Americans is restored, then Europeans in the U.S. will no longer be able to oppress people all around the world. If Europeans in the U.S are no longer able to steal our land, labor and intellectual capital, then they will not be able to compete with the rest of the world. They will have no power. Their system will collapse because it is still based on slavery. If the system of dominance in the U.S. collapses, then the subcontinent of Europe will be confronted with the task of finding a way to survive without dominance. The dominance of the European Diaspora would cease because they have upset just about everyone else in the world with their merciless and monstrous killing.

Black Americans are consigned with the responsibility to remember the fight for sovereignty, which is simply a fight for survival. We must stop accepting the meaningless resistance that has been orchestrated by the oppressor under the guise of civil rights. Humanity's right to self-determination is being threatened. It is not likely that another country will invade Europeans in the U.S. partly because these genocidal maniacs are the only people in the world who have actually used weapons of mass destruction. They used them against the Japanese. An alternative way in which their powerlessness can be exposed is by Black Americans finally unifying to control our own food, clothing and shelter as Elijah Muhammad and others have taught. The oppressor will definitely harass, jail and kill some people if we resist their domination in an attempt at liberation. The fact that we must face is that they harass, jail and kill us anyway. In fact, we lose fewer people when we are fighting back than when we are not fighting for liberation at all. Don't get it twisted. Civil Rights are not liberation. We are critical of this approach because it is vastly incomplete at best. Even worse, it has represented a demented form of freedom that has been an impediment to liberation.

Chapter 2

Re-thinking Slavery and Freedom

LET'S consider a story that nearly everyone knows about as context to explain liberation. As Moses followed spiritual guidance to free his Hebrew people from Egypt, why did he not fight for Civil Rights? It is not a solution to slavery, that's why. Nor did the people rally behind Moses and say Moses run for Pharaoh! Why not? That is also not a solution to slavery. Moses did not lead his people to integrate with the Egyptians. This kind of behavior is pathological. Why would anyone want to integrate with the same people who misuse and abuse them? Alternatively, Moses used a strategy of liberation theology. This is the same strategy that we will share with you. Overall, that is the strategy of this book. We are going to start out like Adam in the Bible with naming things to describe our reality. It is imperative that we embrace our ancestral, spiritual identity as opposed to blindly accepting the oppressor's religious identity that was tortured into our families by the most creatively tortuous methods available. The slaver knows that we can win with our own spiritual identity. He learned this from the story of Moses. This is why the ship on the chess board was changed to a bishop. The invader destroys our spiritual heritage so that we can never become free like the children of Israel. The new slavery is meant to last forever. The bishop does not come to save our souls. He comes to capture our souls so that we will be confined to slavery indefinitely.

We have black people in the U.S. with every academic qualification imaginable and we work in every blue collar field imaginable. We own businesses and we are prolific in sports and entertainment. With these impressively diverse skills, we still cannot seem to devise a solution to liberation so that our children will have the means to survive. Mis-education is not freedom. Integration is not freedom. Civil Rights are not freedom. Emancipation Proclamation is not freedom. We ought to be embarrassed and ashamed to allow our children to be taught such oppressive and humiliating mythology. The year 1865 c.e. was not punctuated by the ending of slavery in the U.S. On the contrary, in fact, it was the beginning of slavery in the U.S. Recall the story of Moses. How did he solve the problem of slavery? He solved it with liberation theology as a means to political independence. Although our situation has been more debilitating, the solution remains the same. There is at least precedent for solving the problem in this way. So what actually happened in 1865? We were not coming together with liberating theology. Nor did we get political independence. Allow us to explain with a brief example.

The history of enslaving horses or dogs is equally as tortuous, although dogs have always been treated much better than Black Americans. Let's assume someone wants to enslave a wild (free) dog. He is going to look for a young impressionable dog. He will not prey on a full grown animal. That would make the dog's conversion less likely. Once he has captured the dog and isolated him from other free dogs, the making of a slave can begin. Many of you are familiar with the Willie Lynch letter regarding the making of a slave. It doesn't matter whether it is true of not. It is relevant to our circumstances. We are using a dog in this example, however, to illustrate techniques used on humans. The slaver has captured a dog and isolated him in his back yard in order to train him to be a slave (pet). He keeps the dog in chains so that he doesn't try to run away and re-join the free dogs. He weans him off of natural foods and never lets him connect to his own food supply so that the dog will be dependent on slave food. He beats the dog whenever he does not comply with the slave training that he is teaching. This is the period of the making of a slave. Once his spirit is broken and he has become fully subjugated, the slave maker can take the chains off. The dog will not run away because now he is a slave. He will also voluntarily teach his children to be slaves.

This example serves as a picture of the transition of 1865 in the U.S. From 1492 to 1865, invading Europeans were in the process of making slaves of their captives in the Americas. By 1865, the process was complete. The indigenous and imported people were fully subjugated and the chains could come off. The torture, terrorism and force feeding were part of the process of making slaves. The destruction of the language and the severance of the people's connection to God was also part of this process of making slaves. By 1865, they could take the chains off. The process was complete. This marked the beginning of slavery. The peaceful people would still be fully governed, dominated and controlled by the slaver. Since the monstrous making of slaves was complete, we were no longer just captives, we had become slaves. We note that Native Americans and Africans successfully fought back the invaders for almost 400 years as in the Seminole Wars that lasted until the 1850s. The resistance to occupation and slavery was effective, but the European diseases and inhumane tactics were undoing. Consequently, the divisions of our families and loss of our identity made organized resistance more difficult. By this time, our freedom was being defined by the Emancipation Proclamation which did not include any spiritual, political or economic independence whatsoever.

It is appalling that we consider ourselves educated and allow our children to be taught that we were made free by an invading slaver. Not only were we not politically independent, we also were not politically integrated. What do we call this state of confusion? We were clearly not citizens of the U.S. What country were we citizens of? It was determined by the slaver's inhumane laws that we could be counted as 3/5 people as long as we were owned as property. The Emancipation Proclamation gave us no protection from former slave owners and no protection from the government. We were not counted as slaves or citizens. Those of you who disagree with the fact that slavery began in 1865; please explain who we were at this time and what group we belonged to. The reality is that we still belonged to the same slaving country that we belonged to in 1860. We were not citizens of any country because we were still slaves. We were not citizens during the period of the making of slaves and we have not been citizens during the period of slavery. Immediately after 1865 repressive organizations began to rise, like the KKK, to ensure that we would never become free or even think about freedom. Schools were built, particularly the 1890 land grant colleges to perpetuate slavery. This was the beginning of mis-education. It was supposed to be a step up from no education. It included private black schools as well. Remember slaves will voluntarily teach their children to be slaves because that is all that they know. Our languages were destroyed, unlike the Hebrews. Our spiritual heritage was destroyed, unlike the children of Israel. This was clearly a new and improved brand of slavery. The new slavery was intended to last forever. In the year 1865, the making of slaves was complete. Slavery was not abolished...it was just beginning.

Let's consider some of the elements of the new slavery that the bishop helped to create. We find from this analysis that Civil Rights, Social Equality and Inclusiveness do not identify the problems that we must solve if we want our children to survive. We must be able to recognize the danger of endless dominance associated with these approaches. Perpetual slavery is one of the causes of the loss of our identity, especially the indigenous part which we will cover later. Blacks in America are still slaves, although the domination has changed names. We must not continue to let the slaver define our reality. We must free ourselves. If we teach our children the truth, then they may get the notion that they should fight for spiritual, political and economic independence. If we continue to allow them to be programmed by oppressive myths, then they will never fight for freedom because they will believe that they are already free. Unfortunately, we have not been teaching our children to think outside of the framework of slavery. We allow and even encourage them to be programmed by the slaver. Then, precariously, we wonder why we are not making any progress as a people.

Our peak social progress was in the 1970's just after the last movement. We became almost 3/5 citizens, yet we have been losing ground ever since then. We have never been more than 3/5 citizens since the European invasion of the U.S. was complete (1890s). Some economically mis-educated people like to refer to the larger black middle class as evidence of progress. This is absolutely meaningless in light of the fact that this just pushed the dominant culture even higher. In reality, we gained no ground in coming out from under oppression. We actually lost ground and repressive tactics increased. Black folks made ten more dollars. Then Europeans in the U.S. made thousands more dollars to oppress us with. What makes us think that this is progress? If a gorilla has great accommodations in the zoo, does that make him free? Of course, it does not. The oppressor defines what slavery is for us; and the oppressor defines what progress is for us since we have not found reasons to be supportive of independent thinking.

The growth of the black middle class does not mean that we have made progress. The growth of black millionaires does not mean that we have made progress. Concern with this position has spawned a book entitled, *Forty Million Dollar Slaves*. We are only commenting on the title. It reminds us of zoo animals who have expensive accommodations. Being confined to the slaver's financial system actually makes us weaker, not stronger. Any of this so-called financial progress can be taken away overnight. They can freeze all of your accounts, throw you in jail, hold you indefinitely, call you a terrorist and there is almost nothing you can do about it. They can do this whenever they want precisely because we are still slaves. We are losing the desire and ability to defend ourselves. We act as if we never heard of the Tulsa race riots. Surely, we have at least seen the movie Rosewood. This was happening all over the country where there was so-called black progress being made. It is also what sparked Claude McKay's poem, *If We Must Die*. Incidentally, black Tulsa has never recovered. Repression followed the destruction.

If we don't know or understand our history, we are doomed to make the same mistakes. We are employing the same fruitless strategies in the new millennium with new names, like economic empowerment. We will cover more on this and the Black Enterprise approach later. For now let's consider the context of the turn of the 20th century. After the beginning of slavery in 1865, prisoner of war schools (Normal schools and HBCUs) began to flourish to perpetuate subjugation. We fought for the chains to come off. We fought for fair prices for our goods and labor. As a result of these successes, we began to rise economically. But because we were still slaves, our progress was watched and regulated. After World War 1, our assumed progress was burned to the ground. Many black men were hanged and burned in the process. Black people will never be allowed to rise as a group as long as we remain under the control of a foreign invading force. What makes us think the oppressor is going to let us rise above him? We apparently do not understand the nature of oppression, not to mention that Eurocentric capitalism is an obvious part of the problem. As our identity crisis is resolved, we will realize that Eurocentric capitalism will never work for the masses of black people regardless of how much manipulated fiat money we acquire. As John Henrik Clarke has said, imitation of the oppressor is not freedom.

Let's consider an anecdote from Malcolm X. Malcolm spoke of these illusions of progress more than forty years ago. We have come further in time as if we did not understand a word that he said. He taught an analogy of progress by speaking of a knife driven six inches into the back of a victim. He said progress is not made just because you have pulled the knife out three inches. In fact progress is not made when the perpetrator pulls the knife all of the way out of the victim's back. Progress is not made until the wound begins to heal. This was the teaching of Malcolm X. I would like to add another dimension to the healing of the wound. The healing of the wound may still be an illusion if the wound is infected. Of course, Malcolm was referring to the dominant culture as the perpetrator with the knife and Black Americans as the wounded victims. To really bring this analogy home, let's assign events to the teaching.

Perhaps 1865 can be seen as pulling the knife out three inches. The 1970s are seen as pulling the knife out all of the way. Now, many Blacks and Europeans in the U.S. seem to think the playing field has been leveled. We all have the same opportunities. Nothing could be further from the truth. This is just more trickery from the Washington Wizards. For example, Europeans in the U.S. had affirmative action policies that worked in their favor from 1619 until about 1969. This is 350 years. Blacks were allowed policies from 1969 until about 1999. This is 30 years. This has been pawned off on our slave consciousness as equality. Our children are taught that everything is equal now. This is some kind of mad magician math. (30 does not equal 350) It does not reflect healing for Black Americans. Unfortunately, the wound still cannot heal because Black Americans have been infected. We have been infected with mis-education, negative images and stereotypes, slave religion, self-destructive capitalism and a host of other viral infections from the psychological warfare unit of European invaders.

The events we assigned seemed to fit the story well, but are still inconsistent with our full analysis. The wound cannot heal until we are spiritually, politically and economically independent. This is the legacy with which we would like to challenge all Black Americans, particularly those who have belief in the story of Moses. We are well aware that Moses did not lead a solution to slavery using tactics of civil rights or integration or running for office of Pharaoh. His strategy involved ancestral religious teachings that lead to political independence. This is the same approach we are taking. Moses' strategy did not condone assimilation into Egyptian culture allowing the people to remain vulnerable to all the tricks of the slaver, including affirmative action. I will explain later how assimilation is a viral infection that will not only keep the wound from healing, but will also kill the body of Black Americans. This is why Moses did not use this strategy. He already knew that it could not work in the long run. It works to benefit the oppressor, not the oppressed. Before we explain how the European invader is a virus, let us explain why he is more than a parasite.

Chapter 3

Behavior of a Virus

BOB Marley sang, "…hypocrites and parasites…"[5] He referred to the dominant culture as parasites because it is obvious the rich feed off of the poor. The upper class feed off of the lower class. Or more specifically, the invading culture feeds off of the indigenous culture, which includes Black Americans in this case. This sets up the parasitic relationship. The problem with the parasite description is that it does not capture the European invader's penchant for total destruction. By the way, Bob Marley did mention this total destruction in a different song. History shows us that Europe has been destroyed so badly in the past that the only arable land and hunting grounds left were for the kings and nobles. This destructive behavior has not changed. This is still the plan. The people in charge know that there are not enough resources for the world to grow economically like the thieves of Europe and the U.S. They don't care. They are continuing to consume and destroy.

The dominant plan is not to save our Mother Earth and thus save ourselves. The plan is to continue to assimilate others into self-destructive Eurocentric culture even though this is accelerating the destruction of the world. Because of a gross mismanagement of resources pawned off as a free market economy, many more poor people will die, while the perpetrators get richer and live like imperious untouchables. Why doesn't the dominant culture care? The reason is that there will still be enough resources left for the top one percent of the people who are controlling the majority of the world's wealth. Everyone else is expendable. This is the sad reality. Of course, devastating illness will accompany this destruction as it has done in Europe before. Apparently, greed is greater than mental clarity. At this point we actually question whether it is possible for the Pan European Diaspora to conceive of a world that is not dominated by self-destructive, genocidal European culture.

It seems as though they would rather set off nuclear bombs than to yield to Mother Nature or yield to more constructive and sustainable practices that non-European people have shown as effective. Something is very wrong with this picture.

We are building a discussion about the causes of our identity crisis, so we are still explaining the far-reaching ramifications of European invasion. It is imperative in restoring our identity that we begin to understand who we are and defend against who we are not. We recognize that we must defend ourselves from foreign invasion, especially from psychological invasion since this is where most of the damage is done. Foreign invasion is more than capturing prisoners of war and enslaving them in the past. Foreign invasion has been continuous against Black Americans in order to perpetuate slavery. It can take on the form of television, radio, video games, school, church, politics, local police, corporations, etc. The virus usually comes in disguise. Otherwise, he would not be able to trick our cells into not destroying him. Of course, once the victim's body is weak enough, the invader no longer needs a disguise. We realize the invader we are dealing with is not a parasite. Parasites feed off of a host; but they do not kill the host. The European Diaspora has made it clear that they will invade, kill and consume until there is nothing left for the majority of people. They are not content with sustainable feeding off of the host. They consume all the life out of the host and look for another one. The people of the Canary Islands are extinct. The people of Tasmania are extinct. There are countless other extinct plants and animals resulting from European invasion. Profit has more appeal than inclusive biodiversity. A parasite does not behave this way. The only creature that behaves this way is a virus.

People of all ethnic backgrounds get fed up with this genocidal behavior. They call the invader a snake, a dog, a swine, a lizard or simply a beast. There is nothing wrong, however, with any of these other creatures. They have their places in Nature, and they do not destroy the world. In an attempt to appear superior to all others, the European has isolated himself as a unique creature. He is uniquely rushing to destroy the world and showing his profound ignorance of Nature. The behavior described is that of a virus, killing indiscriminately without regard to consequences. He feeds off of someone else's life force until he has drained all of the life force out of them and then looks for another host. He forces or tricks healthy cells (people) into behaving just like him and then the whole body is destroyed. The only creature that behaves this way is a virus. A virus turns healthy cells into virus cells, destroys the host and then looks for someone else to invade. In May 2008, it was publicized that this destroyer is looking to invade Mars. He knows he is sucking the life force out of Mother Earth and he is looking for another host.

This discussion is intended to further show the reality of the predator-prey relationship we have with European invaders. It is an attempt to protect ourselves from total destruction. We have to deal with the truth of what is really going on. If we can restore our identity, then we can protect ourselves from a foreign invading virus. Our concern with this issue is that the virus has forced or tricked healthy cells into assimilating or emulating his behavior. Now he can point to others and argue that we behave the same way. He concludes that we must all be the same. We must all be self-destructive by Nature. This is not consistent with reality. Schooling and television are very large parts of this deception. Television, in particular, has been used as a medium in the most wicked sense of the word. The first 'Matrix' movie is an example of the spin put on this issue. The computer people spoke of this human self-destruction. Of course, it was carefully crafted so that the discussion was directed at a black man, Morpheus. This leaves the mind with the image that the black man, in particular, the Black American man is the virus. This is a crafty and pernicious trick. We must learn who we are so that these games cannot be played on our minds, so that the spin doctors cannot effectively spin these tangled webs of deceit. The Black American man has never invaded anyone without being fully controlled by a dominating foreign force. We have never driven anything into extinction. The foreign invading force is the European virus that we call white people. From the perspective of the victim, the European is the invader, the consumer, the harbinger of death. This is written from the point of view of the immune system. Contrary to contemporary mis-education, the foreign invader is not the same as our healthy cells. He is non-self and must be dealt with accordingly in order for us to survive.

Europeans have taught us that they are different from all other humans, superior actually. The empirical evidence suggests something closer to being pale, sickly and dangerous. They are clearly not the same as other humans who do not reject Father Sun and who have love for Mother Earth. They are out of place in the human family which they consider a place of superiority.

The governing bodies of the planet called the G-8 only include Europeans with the exception of Japan. Why? They control the overwhelming majority of the world's wealth. How? Shall we just conclude that it is because they are superior and all other people are inferior? History shows us that they are different, but not necessarily superior. They are currently trying to trick us into believing that we are all the same, yet they do not treat us the same. It is a pure virus game. Nothing in Nature supports this deception. If they really believe we are the same, then why do they hold all other people in the world hostage, particularly Black Americans? If we are the same, why do they treat us like Sean Bell in New York? Why do they treat us like Rodney King? Why do they treat us like we are some other animal if we are not? It should be painfully obvious that we are not the same animal at all. That is why they are so comfortable with treating us like Others.

Television is used to spin another, similar relationship from the European invader to the Black American man. The dominant culture typically projects all of its faults onto the powerless culture. One of these tricks involves predator and prey. This is a very important relationship to understand in order to be able to defend against it. Propaganda in the U.S., especially the news, leads us to believe that Black Americans are the predators and European invaders are innocent of any responsibility or accountability for programming people's behavior. This is the same spin put on the Iraqis as if they are the terrorists. This is bold and unbridled fantasy. In reality, who is terrorizing who? Are Muslims invading the U.S. or is the U.S. invading Muslims? Just look up the definition of terrorism and it will become clear who the terrorist is and who the axis of evil is comprised of. The axis of evil, by definition, is the invading Europeans of the U.S. We are not just referring to the leaders in Washington D. C. It was not the leaders in D.C. who were responsible for hanging black men from trees. Emmett Till was not mutilated and drowned by political leaders. Iraq is not being invaded by congressmen. These kinds of crimes are committed by the common populace. To add insult to injury, we are expected to support murder and torture through supporting our troops.

The common everyday Europeans in the U.S. do not get an innocence pass. They must also be held accountable. They are the ones who drag us behind trucks, rape our women, hang our men, steal our wealth and enslave our children. It may have been European leaders who invaded this land, but it has been the common people who possess it. I do not see them trying to give the land back to the indigenous people. What I do see is them riding around in luxury cars wallowing in the wealth of the indigenous people which they are convinced that they worked for. Fortunately, alternative information is being disseminated more quickly and the psychological spins that used to work against the oppressed are losing their effectiveness. Remember the common European invaders who complained to the U.S. government about the so-called Indians who were invading their land. It was the common everyday people behind the genocidal removal which was coined "the trail of tears." These Europeans who spun the truth were euphemistically called settlers and the Natives were perceived as the invaders. This is an age old spin tactic. It is spun from the exact same web of deceit that is invading Afghanistan and Iraq today. It is also the same web of deceit that paints Black American men as predators.

In reality, the Earth's greatest predator by far is the European invading virus. The prey is any people who do not have nuclear weapons. The prey is Native Americans and Black Americans and Afghans and Iraqis and Africans to name a few. The prey is all the sovereign nations that the U.S. occupies. Predation, however, goes beyond military invasion. For example, who are the perpetrators of predatory lending? This is often practiced in the U.S. against poor people, usually black and undereducated. But it is also practiced internationally by economic hit men. Countries are forced or tricked into debts that they cannot pay. Then their resources are taken and their sovereignty is compromised. The culprits are corporate Europe and corporate U.S. It used to be called the white power structure. In understanding our identity crisis, we must recognize that the virus is a predator and that we have become the unnatural prey. We cannot deny a predator-prey relationship with the dominant culture. This is the uncomfortable reality. We do not have a "we are all the same" relationship. Convincing us that we are the same just makes us easier prey. It is analogous to virus cells infiltrating the body by tricking the healthy cells into believing that the virus cells are the same. This stops the immune system from destroying the virus and the result, if unchecked, is death.

Some readers may consider this discussion divisive. Our reply to that is simply, what happens if we allow the foreign invading force to go unchecked? What happens when we allow it to infiltrate the body? As you already know, it will turn the healthy cells into virus cells until it takes over the body and destroys it. This is exactly what is happening to Black Americans and the Earth. We do not understand who we are; therefore we do not know what is foreign. As a result, we cannot protect ourselves from foreign invasion. We are not able to recognize the subtleties and nuances of that which is harmful. This leaves us headed for destruction. Recognition is the first step in problem solving. We will cover the other steps of how to defend from the virus at the end of this section. For now, let's look at some general steps to problem solving. Dr. White, whose teachings are the foundation for nearly half of this book, gave us four steps which he summarized from M.L.K's letter from the Birmingham jail. Those steps are Recognition, Dialogue, Purification and Direct Action. We have been on the verge of recognizing the real problems in the past. Unfortunately the beatings, jailing, killing and death threats have caused us to abandon fighting for our human right to be free in favor of the safer, prescribed struggle for civil rights and social equality of the 'prominent black leader' variety.

One goal of this book is to suggest that there is more to remember and to recognize as a first step in solving our collective problem of oppression. We offer an unassimilated view of the impediments to freedom. Our approach contrasts with but does not conflict with the symptomatic prescriptions of some of our prominent black leaders. We build on our relieved symptoms to work for cures to the unsolved problem of slavery. In order to develop a viable strategy to solve this problem, it is necessary for us to realize who we are and who we must defend ourselves from. Let's turn our attention back to the identity crisis and take a look at some issues having to do with the pale man. We will elucidate a description that Elijah Muhammad included in his book entitled, *Message to the Black Man*. It was mentioned that the so-called white man was grafted out of the black man. This is not consistent with a layman's understanding of albinism. We are not scientific experts on albinism. We can, however, think logically enough to determine that a black albino is not a European just because he is pale with blue eyes. Albinism is an illness or birth defect, but it does not change a person into an entirely different creature. It does not make his nose more aquiline or his lips disappear. It does not make his hair straighten out or his muscles change form. That "old pale thing" that Malcolm X referred to was not a black albino. It was the European invader.

Who have black albinos invaded? What have they destroyed? Two black Albinos cannot make a European baby…now or in the past. In stark contrast to the behavior of passive black albinos, Europeans have brought to the Americas an extreme and unprecedented destructiveness. Bolivian President, Evo Morales, has even described the actions of the dominant culture as anti-life policies in a Newsweek web exclusive. (Apr. 2008) Along these same lines, we recently saw a young male of European descent on an internet video making fun of President Bush. In his skit, he said that Bush wanted Nature to conform to the Bush administration's agenda. This very much summarizes the mindset that controls the behavior of the general majority of Europeans in the U.S. Some may give lip service to organic farming or energy conservation; but for the most part, the dominant culture refuses to admit that the entire industrial revolution was an uncivilized blunder. It is the same as not admitting to the uncivilized behavior in Iraq. The industrial revolution was simply designed to further the causes of white supremacy and global domination. It is the result of a lack of understanding and respect for Nature. It foolishly assumes that they can fight against Nature and win. The leaders in the U.S. are still so committed to Nature-destroying economic growth that they continue to sell this anti-life behavior to so-called developing nations. In fact, it is being forced on the world disguised as democracy and free market economics.

Obviously, Black Americans are not the only ones whom Europeans are indefinitely subordinating. As demonstrated by their actions, their practice is that all living things must submit to their domination or die. There is no need for a conspiracy. The normal working of this culture destroys all other living things. This is how we arrive at descriptions like anti-life. We offer sustainable descriptions of self and non-self so that all people can have a future. We must accurately identify predator and prey. Knowledge of self is more clearly understood in conjunction with knowledge of Nature. This is an introduction to our first solution. The more we understand of the Laws of Nature, the less vulnerable we will be to the tricks of the oppressor. We will also look at some spiritual solutions, rooted in an understanding of Nature, which will help to take away our fear. The European invading terrorists control us with fear. Their strategy is to mercilessly destroy any attempt at freedom. This is part of a pre-emptive strategy. Just because you have European friends, do not be fooled into thinking that they are not complicit with your destruction. If they like you so much, ask them to help you establish a political entity independent of their domination. Only then can we come to the table as equals. As it used to be said, 'God blessed the child who has his own.' European invaders only like you when you stay in your subordinated place. Begin fighting for freedom and see what happens. You will get the same response that a healthy cell gets from a virus.

Getting back to understanding who we are, let's take another look at color, since we were discussing albinism. W.E. B. Dubois wrote many years ago that the problem of the 20th century was the problem of a color line. Based on what we have identified about albinism, this is not altogether true. The trickster has taught us to define people by color, but this is not an accurate or liberating way of describing people. We have seen that a black albino is pale with kinky hair. Is his color black? No. Is he European? No. He may be pale like a European, but he is not a European. Nor will he ever be treated like a European because of his kinky hair. The problem here cannot be color since a European and a black albino are the same color, or lack thereof. It would be more reasonable to suggest the problem is with kinky hair. Even this is inadequate because Black Americans, including Black American albinos are different from Europeans from head to toe, not just with hair. In addition to explaining paleness, allow us to offer a short explanation of why this book will not give any credence to the description of a white man or white people. The naming of things and the associated connotations and imagery are a large part of the problem with the combination of psychological dominance and slavery.

The color white is associated with notions of purity and angels. The description of pale is associated with notions of being sickly and half baked. Based on the historical and current behavior of the Pan-European Diaspora, the latter designation fits the reality. When Malcolm X referred to Europeans in the U.S. as "that old pale thing", he was not spewing venomous hate. He was classifying and observed reality. The torture, terrorism and repression of his time made it clear to Malcolm that he was not fighting against a white man. He was fighting against a pale, sickly and dangerous creature. Describing people by color mis-identifies who we are and who the foreigner is. We will refrain from using the pale man description for Europeans in the U.S. because it could be confused with albinos who have kinky hair. The albino has an illness that apparently involves melanin. The European is also pale, but he suffers from an additional illness. His illness is played out as total destruction. On this issue, we find the academic position, the Afrocentric position and Elijah Muhammad's position to be misleading. Africans did not evolve into Europeans; nor were they from an Albino clan or grafted from Africans by a genetic scientist. What we do know is that they behave like viruses and we do not know where they came from.

We have to appreciate the sacrifices made by some 'whites' who have struggled on the side of oppressed people in the U.S. and abroad. The immediate benefit can often be life sparing or prison sparing. We take our current position on defining the invasion process for ourselves because there are other consequences to be considered in assessing the full scope of foreign aggression. The opposing behavior on the part of a minority of whites effectively puts the aggressive foreigner on both sides of the invasion. It tends to confuse the victims and ultimately makes them more vulnerable to the destructive process of the overwhelming majority of the foreign invading group. The victims become less able to define self and non-self which translates to being less able to defend themselves.

Much of the historical assistance brought to indigenous and invaded people has been by invading clergy members who assume a religious responsibility. This also has consequences typically not considered. Often this process of protection comes with Christianizing the family, which turns out to be another front of the invasion. And this is from the whites who love you and protect you. This is not to say that there is necessarily malicious intent with all invasive religious conversion. In the end, however, religious results are disastrous. The identity crisis is worsened as more parts of the culture are dismantled. Religious conversion is part of that dismantling. In reality, there is not much, if anything, that a foreign invader can teach indigenous people about spirituality. Conversion actually decreases our ability to survive because it fills our spiritual cup with toxic foreign material. We find our spirit where we find our bodies and the bodies of our ancestors. We have our own credible creation stories from around the Southern Atlantic, including the Caribbean. It takes a spiritual, introspective journey to solve the problem of an identity crisis and thus gain the necessary power to overcome modern day slavery in the U.S.A.

There have also been invaders compelled by moral responsibility and have given their lives to helping the oppressed with health care and education, to mention just a couple of areas. The argument here is that they generally cannot teach us our healing methods. They cannot educate us in our ways of doing things or teach us who we are. They will not teach us our language or religious practices. The best attempt is to make us poorly performing European type creatures. Since we recognize all invaders are not immediately harmful or malevolent, we work with those who are willing to help us survive because they recognize the value of our independent existence. We work with those who love themselves and their children enough to recognize the need to listen to indigenous methods of sustainability. We are not suggesting that all people of any group act in the same way. We are, however, making it clear who self is and who non-self is. We are also not equivocal in our understanding and description of the foreign invading virus.

We respect the right of the invader to live. We simply encourage him to learn to live independently of other people's land, labor and resources. Invaders become more human as well when political, military and economic controls are restored to indigenous and oppressed people. In this scenario, invaders learn to stand on their own two feet without being dependent on stealing and destroying others, like a virus. All of humanity is improved in this process.

Chapter 4

To Steal, Kill and Destroy

THE totally destructive and anti-life behavior of the European Diaspora explains why people like Elijah Muhammad and others engender ideas about a blue-eyed devil. More recently, invaded Arab nations have referred to the leaders in D.C. as the Great Satan. Also, at a recent United Nations meeting, Hugo Chavez of Venezuela called George Bush the Devil. Why would different countries at different times all refer to Europeans as devils, or the equivalent name of Satan? In the Americas, this idea of Devil comes from the Bible. So, let's look at what the Bible has to say about it. In John 10:10, the scripture refers to the thesis of the literature and its anti-thesis. In the New Testament, the thesis is Jesus, while the anti-thesis is the Devil. The scripture reads, "the thief cometh not but for to steal, kill and destroy, but I am come that you might have life and have it more abundantly." The anti-thesis referred to is the Devil. The Devil's behavior is clearly described. What did Europeans do when they entered Africa besides steal, kill and destroy? Obviously, they did the same thing when they invaded the Americas. What are they still doing in Afghanistan and Iraq in 2008? They are stealing, killing and destroying. It is no mystery why people all over the world see the European Diaspora as devils.

The U.S. was built on foundations of stealing, killing and destroying. According to the Bible, the founding fathers were devils. The only way that we can possibly think otherwise is if the European Diaspora stops stealing, killing and destroying all over the world to force people to make them rich. Or we can just ignore the facts as most of us do. We have noticed unchanged and unmitigated behavior over time. It has nothing to do with blue eyes or pale skin. This behavior is a result of a poison mentality that thinks freedom means they can steal from whomever they want, kill whomever they want and destroy whatever they want. This is especially obvious if they are looking for gold, oil or diamonds. It is again imperative that we begin to understand what the real problems are so that we can begin to defend ourselves and survive. Total destruction is not acceptable. Genocide is not acceptable. We must have certain information in order to have a future. We have to understand how Nature works and, therefore, will be able to recognize what works against Nature. Clarity in this area will enable us to secure a place in this world for our children. In this writing, we are not exactly associating Europeans with devils because we don't actually believe in the Bible concept of the Devil. The Popol Vuh of the Quiché Maya does a better job of describing the antithesis as the Lords of Xibalba (tricksters). We will cover more on this in the section on spirituality. In terms of understanding non-self through knowledge of self, we are discussing the thief and the victim, the murderer and the dead, the destroyer and the damaged.

The foreign invading virus we are dealing with in the U.S. is typically in disguise. He is historically disguised as an explorer. His exploration was a disguise for stealing, killing and destroying. He is disguised as an economic developer. The result is the same. He is disguised as a liberator, but he is a slaver. He is disguised as spreading democracy, but he is spreading a viral infection that is destroying the world. It is going to take a clear and logical understanding of reality and relationships in order to solve these problems. It is clear that the spin doctors in U.S. politics have named an axis of evil to describe those who will not willingly submit to their destructive global domination. The problem is not just that they want to rule the world. The problem is that they are destroying all life forms in the process, to include themselves. The prevailing line of thinking is that if you disagree with them, then you must be evil. Ezra Aharone, in his book entitled, *Pawned Sovereignty*, wrote, "Up until this very day, they believe their positions are always right and best for everyone…"[6] Their behavior makes it clear that they are not trying to be the same as Black Americans, or any other people for that matter. They have no intention of ever leveling the playing field. They are not trying to abolish perpetual slavery and oppression. What remains the same is the age old dominance that has been in place since we were overcome by their illnesses.

There is nothing the same between Black Americans and European invaders, except that we are both bipeds. The gene game, the DNA game and the human race game are just tricks to dig us into a deeper hole. We are not different races. We are different animals entirely. It is insightful here to consider the root and etymology of the word mulatto. The root word is mule. The interesting thing about a mule is that it comes from two very different parents. They can mate, which means they are in the same species, but they are not the same animal. One is a horse and the other is a donkey. Just as the parents of the mule are different animals, the parents of a mulatto are also two different animals. Otherwise, they would not have called the offspring a mulatto. The parents are different animals, not different races. Mulatto can refer to a European and Native American offspring or it can refer to a European and African offspring. For more insight on this language, read *Africans and Native Americans* by Jack Forbes. Just because two creatures can mate does not mean that they are the same animal. This simply means that they are in the same species. The problem we are identifying with the invader and the invaded is not a racial problem. It is a problem between two different animals. Black Americans do not have the same genes as Europeans even though many are tainted with this blood.

From the union of these gene pools, the invader created the description of mulatto. The European Diaspora has isolated and separated itself as a separate superior group, above all other gene pools of humans. We are definitely different, but that does not make one superior to the other. Since we have been discussing the mulatto, consider what would happen if we take a minority of horses and force them to live with donkeys. Would they appear as inferior? Would they be miserable as they were forced to fit into donkey culture under the disguises of integration and diversity? Would they ever actually fit into donkey culture? The end result for the horses would likely be extinction, particularly if the donkeys tortured and terrorized the horses for hundreds of years. Genocide would definitely result if the donkeys erased the horses' memory of how to be horses. As a Black American parallel, we will assume they also erased their identity and taught them that they were the same as donkeys except that they were inferior. But what would happen if the horses' identity was restored? Would they remain subordinate to the donkeys, or would they create their own society based on horse endowments? This example just serves to illustrate Native Americans and Africans living under the foreign invading rule of Europeans. It serves to illustrate that racism is not the problem. We are different animals biologically, culturally and socially.

Relatively small amounts of mixture do not immediately or automatically dilute the stark differences between self and non-self.

Some Black Americans have been so victimized that we make comments like, 'I don't see color.' Our typical response is that maybe you don't but the oppressor does. That is why he is kicking your son's behind in the street every night and prostituting your daughter at every available opportunity. We don't see much of anything except what we are trained to see by the slaver. He said, 'don't eyeball me boy.' So, we do not actually look at the invader and take notice that he is foreign. This is what allows a virus to infiltrate and destroy. While we are bowing our heads in inferiority or turning the other cheek, this creature is killing our people dead and painting the picture as if we are doing it to ourselves. We follow the slave programming that we are inundated with every day. We are bombarded with something on the order of 30,000 messages per day. If we do not begin to de-program now, we will not survive. We will share some basic facts to help us along this journey of differentiating between self and non-self. In this way, we can protect ourselves from the invasion of non-self. This will also speak directly to the slave mentality that says I don't see color, which is really just to say that I am unwilling to defend myself against foreign invasion.

Consider my hair. It is kinky. The European invader does not have kinky hair. Let's go from head to toe and see if we can identify anything that is the same. Not only is my hair different, my head is also shaped differently. My head is flat. I can carry a basket on my head. The invader typically has more of a cone head. Years ago, the Saturday Night Live show used to do a skit called the Cone Heads which was based on this observation. My eyes are also different. They may be light-colored underneath, but they have a darker brown covering. My ears are different. Black people typically have smaller ears. Speaking of ears, have you ever seen Barbara Walters on television? Of course, our noses are larger and broader. You have probably noticed the defacing of artifacts in Africa and America as an attempt to hide the presence of black people. Our lips are not the same either. Apparently a full set of lips is more attractive since European women in the U.S. get shots in their lips in order to make them thicker. So far, all we have covered is the head and everything is different.

Let's start just below the head. Our vocal chords are different. It is confusing in the presence of a growing number of mulattos, but the black female on average has a deeper voice than the male of European descent. The bass in our voices is one of the reasons why black men were encouraged to use falsetto voices in much of the popular music since the civil rights era. This was just another attack on the masculinity of the black man. Our arms and legs are not the same either. We have a different torso to appendages ratio. For the layman, our arms and legs are longer. When we are allowed to eat human foods, are waists are smaller while our hips are larger, at least for the women. I will not even get started on the buttocks. The difference here has been grossly over-advertised. Our muscles are made differently, which is most obvious in the legs. We have short belly muscles with long tendons. Europeans have long belly muscles with short tendons. This is why he typically cannot jump as high or run as fast. He has very little leverage with that short tendon. It is like being on the short side of a see-saw. Because of our muscle and bone structure, we are swift like the cat. The European runs long but not fast like the dog. We also have flatter feet which includes a heel. Europeans have a less defined heel, which is why they put a heel on the shoe.

We can put our scientific blinders on and recant, like Tony Brown, that there are only six genes that separate us. The truth is that we have almost nothing in common. What we are trying to do is help us recognize what is true as opposed to having blind faith in scientific belief. Eurocentric science is always designed to support white supremacy. At this point in time, teaching that we are all the same is beneficial to forwarding the goals of white supremacy. To quote Aharone again, this "…fabricated sameness has not unified us with Euro-Americans or with ourselves."[7] When we say, we don't see color, we are saying that we do not see ourselves as important enough to have an identity separate from what the oppressor has imposed or designated. We think we are dark skinned white people. It pleases the slaver for us not to look at him. As in the Rodney King case he might say, don't believe your lying eyes. As it has been made clear by this analysis, color is not what is important. We must recognize that Black Americans and European invaders are two entirely different animals. We don't see the same colors. We don't smell the same. We don't have the same tastes. We don't hear the same sounds. We don't move the same. When it comes to dancing, we obviously move to the beat of a different drum.

We accept the idea of sameness from the dominating community at large because it makes us more acceptable to them. The problem with this is that acceptance by the oppressor does not improve our survivability. If a monkey behaves as the zookeeper expects, then he may improve his conditions inside of the zoo. He may get better food and better accommodations, but this does not improve his ability to survive. As a captive, he is at the mercy of the zookeeper and his life span will be shortened. His survivability is only improved if he can learn the ways of freedom and get out of the zoo. Even then, without knowledge of self, he will not likely survive. He must overcome the identity crisis of being a zoo animal. This example illustrates the experience of Black Americans confined to the framework of modern U.S. slavery. We are confined in every way by someone who doesn't belong here in the first place. A European is not an American. Europeans invaded America. Calling themselves Americans is more of the virus trick that works to destroy the body of Indigenous Americans. This part is obvious. What is less obvious is that this destruction of Indigenous Americans includes Black Americans. What we are saying is that like a virus, they have stolen our identity so that they can live and we will die as they pursue other hosts. Remember that virus cells invade and trick your body into believing that they are the rightful tenants of your body. The invading virus cells multiply like Europeans multiplied in America. They start so-called Indian schools and HBCUs to turn indigenous cells into virus cells. The end result is that the whole body is destroyed.

If we call the foreign invading force by name, it takes away his power. He is not an American by any stretch of the imagination. He is a European. Allow us to use another illustration from the larger animal family. Let's use a polar bear as an analogy. If a polar bear is moved to the Miami zoo, does it become a Miami bear? Of course it doesn't. And to understand the nature of this creature and its behavior, we must be clear on its identity as a polar bear even though it lives in Florida. Likewise, if an Asian elephant is moved to the Miami zoo, it does not become an American elephant. Following this logic, we find that a European does not become an American by virtue of invading America. Quite the opposite is the reality. Europeans occupy the Americas with foreign military force. By definition, this is the Occupied United States and Occupied America. This is not new Europe. The Americas do not belong to Europeans and Europeans do not belong in America. We can be sure of this just as we can be sure the polar bear does not belong in the Miami zoo. The naming of things is very important. To quote Jan Carew again in *Fulcrums of Change*, "To rob people or countries of their names is to set in motion a psychic disturbance which can in turn create a permanent crisis of identity."[8]

Expect this book to name things as they are seen by the oppressed victims of European invasion. It has already been mentioned that we do not see things in the same way as the invader. The important thing is that we begin to see and to name things in a way that is consistent with truth as verified or validated by the laws of Nature. This stands in direct opposition to Eurocentric beliefs which work against Nature. Unfortunately, as the virus traveled West across the Atlantic, it mutated into an even more destructive form. It was not just Europeans who invaded the Americas. It was European greed-mongers and European poor, or more commonly known as white trash. This may sound like an insult, but it actually is not information that originates with us. This is proudly graven and displayed by European invaders on a bronze plaque at the Statue of Liberty. The poem written by Emma Lazarus and displayed for the world, gives us unambiguous framework for what is meant by liberty in the U.S. The message means freedom for white trash. Wretched refuse means trash. There is no way around this. So that our words are not mistaken for pointless insults, read the following inscription for yourself:

"Not like the brazen giant of Greek fame,
With conquering limbs astride from land to land;
Here at our sea-washed, sunset gates shall stand
A mighty woman with a torch, whose flame
Is the imprisoned lightning, and her name
Mother of Exiles. From her beacon-hand
Glows world-wide welcome; her mild eyes command
The air-bridged harbor that twin cities frame.
"Keep ancient lands, your storied pomp!" cries she
With silent lips. "Give me your tired, your poor,
Your huddled masses yearning to breathe free,
The wretched refuse of your teeming shore.
Send these, the homeless, tempest-tost to me,
I lift my lamp beside the golden door!"[9]

Emma Lazarus

There are no uncertain terms explaining who the Statue of Liberty stands for. It stands for the freedom of European trash to abuse, enslave and murder any other people in the process of naming and claiming liberty. This is not ancient history. This rubbish is still being perpetuated in the new millennium. Operation Enduring Freedom in Afghanistan and Operation Iraqi Freedom in Iraq are testaments to the European idea of liberty in the U.S. Obviously, this creature has a very demented view of liberty. Every European country with the wherewithal came to the Americas to steal, kill and destroy. There was so much stealing from paradise that some countries acquired world changing amounts of loot just by stealing from other Europeans, who stole from the Americas. England was one such country. This is how they eventually gained control of the U.S. The U.S. is occupied by a foreign military force made up of many European countries; but it is controlled by the English. The English gained control largely as a result of piracy and other ruthless, skull and bones tactics.

England would have us believe that her Navy was superior and that she was a tactical genius like Popeye the cartoon character. When you are destroying life and the living, what is the likelihood that you are going to tell the truth about it? All of the history of the U.S. is pure fantasy. These fantasies are played out in the heart warming pirate movies that are shown to every generation of children as part of their assimilation programming. Piracy is not only taught to be acceptable, it is actually programmed in such a way that children grow up with a fondness of piracy. Pirates, with the famous skull and bones symbol, came to steal, kill and destroy. The Bible describes this as the Devil. Let us remember that this is not just an historical reality. This is an ongoing reality that is played out in the Middle East and elsewhere today. It has been reported that the Bush family is still part of the skull and bones organization. They continue to steal, kill and destroy in full view of the public as the common people are directed to blindly support our troops. In this society, pirates are lauded and perceived as desirables. Every generation is programmed with a heroic view of pirates because this is how England wrested control of the U.S.

There is plenty of information on the truth about pirates. As mentioned, the invader cannot and will not tell the truth about the invasion, so you must go to the indigenous sources to get a broader picture. *Indian Givers* by Jack Weatherford is one such source. In order to get a clear picture of the invasion of the Americas, *Conquest of Paradise* by Kirkpatrick Sale is also a must read. In order to understand the causes of our identity crisis, we need to have a thorough understanding of the European invasion of the Americas. The insatiable greed of the aggressor has no limits when it comes to gaining control of resources and people. The mind set is one of global domination. One of the things we must understand about the superiority complex of the aggressor is that he will never treat anyone as equals. We have already worked our way through a discussion about sameness. Our analysis concluded that fighting for social equality is futile. This is why our struggle for freedom in the 1960s was changed into a struggle for social equality. In this way, we would never actually make any progress. The dominant culture has no intention of making it possible for others to compete with their wealth and control. They do not have a mind set of survival. They have a mind set of total control. They will destroy the entire planet just to gain control of it.

Let us re-phrase that. They ARE destroying the whole world in order to control it. This is beyond black and white. It is beyond a white and non-white issue. Even among themselves, there is always jockeying for central, minority control. As far as our identity is concerned, we are wired for much flatter governance. We are not made up for hierarchal control. In thinking about European's unilateralist nature, I am reminded of a television program from about a decade ago. A program called "48 hours," showed a time in Europe when women mostly took care of healing their families. This program also showed the violent transition where men took control. The women were abused and burned alive for applying ancestral and herbal techniques. They were designated as witches as the men took control of medicine with so-called modern techniques. Of course the modern techniques were unnatural although seemingly more rational. This was essentially the beginning of modern medicine where chemicals are used to treat symptoms while cures for the whole person are often ignored.

European men killed their own women to take control of medicine and health care. In the process of making slaves, like Black Americans, this is also one of the areas that remain under strict control. Consider that there are a great number of Jewish doctors in the U.S. Why? Jews have no intention of ever becoming slaves again. You must control your healthcare to keep from being dominated by the slaver. We only brought up the "48 hours" program to illustrate that Europeans do not even allow equality among themselves. So, what makes us think that they will ever allow Black Americans to be equals? It will never happen. Equality is hopeful nonsense fed to us to keep us spinning our wheels with more of the 'gradualism' strategy. Our desire for equality is still being placated by token Negroes. If they will destroy their own women to gain control, they will certainly destroy us to maintain control. With the same mindset, they are destroying Mother Earth to gain control. Instead of following her lead, they are trying to force her to comply with their demands. The problem with this is that Mother Earth is not a European woman. Contrary to the Bible scripture in the book of Genesis chapter 1, she cannot be subdued. This is not a battle that Europeans or any other people can win.

Our recent strategy has been to take up no battle for survival at all because we have been effectively reduced and confined to a superficial fight for equality. We follow the same scripted fights by sold out leaders that Alton Maddox Jr. has spoken about. This creates the illusion that black people in the U.S. are actually fighting for something useful. In reality, we are not fighting for survival at all. We are fighting to become equal and unified with invasive, destroyers. Confined in the mind and soul, we continue to be played as if life is a game. We continue to allow the invader to gradually take us into extinction. The strategy of gradualism that M.L.K spoke about in his "I Have a Dream" speech is still a major problem today. The oppressor always uses gradualism to allow incremental but circular change. Our expectation of equality is without historical precedent. If we remain mired in this rut of dependence, we will be slaves of the invader until the end of humanity. We accept this future for our children because of ignorance, fear and laziness. Hundreds of years of European torture and terrorism have negatively affected our desire and ability to fight for freedom. So, we keep hope alive as Jesse Jackson taught and remain victims of gradualism. Bob Marley sang, "some people have hopes and dreams; some people have ways and means."[10] In order to survive, we will have to overcome the hopes of Jesse Jackson and the dreams of M.L.K. We will have to establish independent ways and means.

The Western European capitalist system that we live in is designed to exploit the poor and underprivileged which are mostly black people and others of color. As we think we are acquiring ways and means, it turns out to only be the ways and means of the oppressor and we become exploiters of our own people in the process. One of the most notable examples is Bob Johnson. Using Black Entertainment Television, he sold out an entire generation of black youth irrespective of parental intervention. Then we further glorify self hate by exalting him as a great businessman. Of course, it is not just Bob Johnson. Greed over need is the way our imposed system operates. The entire U.S. corporate structure is in the business of exploiting indigenous lands and people for profit. In our case, the indigenous exploited people have been infused with displaced Africans. Economically, we have been assimilated into this system and learned to be viruses ourselves.

It is unfortunate that our problem is not only external oppression, but also our problems with survival have been internalized. A good literary resource on this subject is *Killing Rage* by bell hooks (We are not disrespecting her by spelling her pen name in lower case. This is her creative preference). Actually, anything that you can get by bell hooks is worth reading. She is a very powerful resource. We have internalized and become complicit with stealing, killing and destroying as it has become a normal part of our lives. This is destructive whether we point the finger at European invaders or emulate this behavior ourselves. The problem is correctable as we begin to name and define things for ourselves.

Chapter 5

Defining the Box

WHILE the cause of our identity crisis is external, the crisis itself is internal. For this reason, it is important to discuss one of the powerful insights of bell hooks. In paraphrase, she has suggested that every institution in the U.S. promotes and maintains white supremacist capitalist patriarchy. If you are black in the U.S., this doesn't require any research. All you have to do is turn on your T.V. or the radio or walk outside of your door. The institutionalized racism described by bell hooks is ubiquitous in this country. As a result, it is internalized by all people reared in this system. It is beneficial to Europeans in the U.S.; but it is detrimental to the survival of black people in this country. The works of bell hooks are always inspirational. Her incredible analysis led us to a defining reality. Dr. White used to always teach us that we must define our terms in order for dialogue to be useful. In this instance, we realized that bell hooks had defined the box. She had given us four sides. Since we are defining the box specifically, we had to modify her argument slightly. We have already mentioned another important book to read entitled, *Pawned Sovereignty* by Ezra Aharone. He writes of the founding pillars of this country being weaponized Democracy, Capitalism and Euro-Christianity. Combining the insights of these powerful minds, we can define the four sides of the box clockwise as follows:

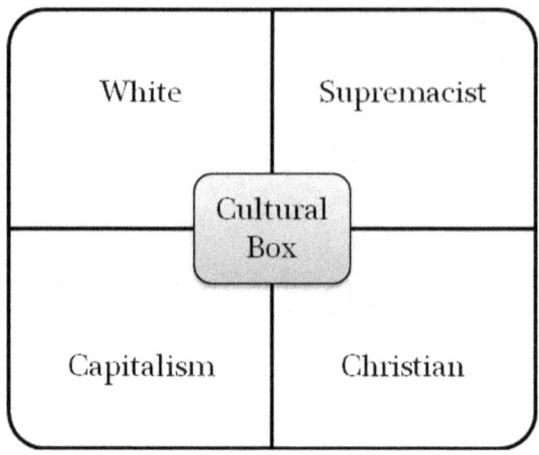

We often speak in this country about thinking outside of the box. In building on the arguments of bell hooks and Ezra Aharone, I argue that we can define the box in the diagram above as White-Supremacist-Christian-Capitalism. This does not exclude bell hooks' insight on patriarchy. It turns out that patriarchy is embedded within Christianity. The concept that the box does not include is Democracy. We are defining reality so that the truth can make us free. We are not dealing with fantasy and fiction. This country is not a democracy, nor has it ever been a democracy since European invasion. This is a Republic. It is an Aristocracy. It is an Oligarchy. There are other terms that can be used to describe this governing structure; but it cannot be truthfully described as a Democracy of any kind. If we refer back to *Indian Givers* by Jack Weatherford, or to *The Southeastern Indians* by Charles Hudson, we will find that this was a Participatory Democracy before the invasion. The foreign invading forces copied only those parts of the indigenous governing structure that would give the illusion of Democracy. We have long since known that truth can make us free, yet we internalize all of these untruths and then wonder why we cannot achieve freedom.

In beginning to think outside of the box, we first look at the terms that define the box. The only side of the box that we have discussed at length is the fact that Europeans in the U.S. are not white. We defined this part of the box as a pale sickly and dangerous foreign devilish virus. More than 500 years of historical and contemporary data in the West make this description unquestionably clear. We can question any indigenous people in the world that Europeans have invaded and we will invariably get the same descriptive response, albeit in another language. If we can get this far, we have at least begun to think outside of the box. Moving counterclockwise, the next side of the box is Supremacist. We briefly covered the Divine right to rule the world and the superiority complex established from the Hebrew and Christian Holy Scripture. We will further develop an understanding of non-hierarchal structures as we move through the following chapters. For now, let's just recognize that in a boxed in world constructed by Europeans, there is necessarily hierarchal control. In the real world of Nature, which is a sphere, there is no top and bottom. Since there is no top, there is no superior, no supreme. Since there is no bottom, there are no inferiors, no subordinates. A queen bee is not a queen.

The third side, the Christian side of the box is labeled as such because this is the religion that was used in the invasion of the Americas. It is of paramount importance to realize that Christianity is part of the invasion, oppression and perpetual slavery. It is not a solution. It is part of the problem. In other words, it is anti-liberating. Christians invaded and enslaved Black Americans. Christians did not free us. Beliefs will keep us in the box and keep us enslaved. The truth, using facts and the laws of Nature, will make us free. Given that Islam and Judaism are also very patriarchal, these religions are also problematic for the liberation of Black Americans. The Christian side of the box includes Judaism and Islam. These religions may be okay in the Middle East, but they are inappropriate and destructive in the Americas. They bring desert rules to the forest. We will cover more on this in the chapter on spirituality. One thing we should mention in favor of Islam is that it seems to recognize the evils of compound interest, which brings us to the next side of our box. The interest component of Western European Capitalism brings out the worst in people and is destroying our lifeline (Mother Earth) for profit. Debt driven free market economics is just another way that European invaders are forwarding the cause of white supremacy as they move toward global domination. They invade initially with the military and perpetuate the invasion with economics.

Our opposite economic identity is best described by communalism. If we can learn to think in terms of our own identity, then we will find that sharing is much more efficient than exploitation. Communalism is outside of the box and completely outside of the current educational system, which makes it ripe for innovation rather than innovation stifling. This kind of thinking does not lend itself to global domination. In the current schooling process, even our critical thinking skills are guided through careful programming to remain inside of the box. We have to challenge ourselves and our peers to think outside of the well crafted box. Reading more bell hooks can help us overcome issues with patriarchy and help transform our relationships and family life. Keep in mind that matriarchy is not a solution to patriarchy. Developing a balanced, non-patriarchal mentality is the goal. Shared power structure is not foreign to the Americas. This was the practice prior to foreign invasion. Being unable to think outside of the box leaves us in a condition similar to zoo animals. This boxed in framework is spiritual and mental while it perpetuates our physical slavery. Let's summarize what we have covered thus far regarding the results of European invasion.

One of the results of the invasion of this part of North America is that we became prisoners of war in what is now the U.S. Less than half a million captured Africans were brought to the U.S. Captured Native Americans along with these few captured Africans became prisoners of war. These Native children were separated from any indigenous roots so that they could be reduced to inputs of economic production. The functioning of Western European Capitalism and the presumed progress of European expansion involves the full exploitation of the land, labor and intellectual capital of mostly indigenous people. The exploitation of prisoner capital is called slavery. Through this process, we have lost our identity. In order to restore our identity, we need to make sure that we understand the process of making a slave so that we can reverse it. The following outline identifies cycles of U.S. slavery:

1492-1865	**Agrarian (Plantation) Slavery**	
	The making of spiritual, emotional and physical slaves	
Methods:	1) Separation from indigenous spirituality	
	2) Torture and separation from culture	
1865-1964	**Industrial Slavery**	
	Characterized by the making of mental slaves	
Methods:	1) Mis-education using illusions of freedom	
	2) More productive slaves increases dominance	
1964-1992	**Information Slavery**	
	Characterized by the making of perpetual slaves	
Methods:	1) Media manages resistance	
	2) Psychological control using illusions of progress	
1992-Present	**New Millennium Slavery**	
	Characterized by the completion of perpetual slavery	
Methods:	1) Fully disconnect from food supply	
	2) Remove means to liberation	

There are countless books on slavery in the U.S. This summary is not intended to be an exhaustive list of methods or a perfect description of dates and terms. The idea put forth here is that we are still dealing with a problem that we have never solved. The reason we find yet another reference to slavery is that apparently we still do not understand the nature of the problem. We must understand the poison in order to create the antidote. Actually, we must understand Nature to create a successful antidote. The outline above summarizes the fact that we have become perpetual slaves. The problem that we must solve is not one of civil rights or social justice. The problem is that we are perpetual slaves and we have a human right to be free. We have never achieved spiritual, political and economic independence; therefore, we are still slaves. One of the reasons we cannot solve the problem is because we are approaching the problem as if we are already free. We are using a solution set that does not reflect the reality of the problem. If the problem asks for the sum of 2+2, then what good is a solution set of {6,7,8,9}? We end up with impossible solution sets because we continue to let the creator of the problem define our past, present and future. It has been said many times before, the slaver cannot emancipate us. Stop allowing our children to be programmed with this insidious information. We must define the problem for ourselves. This is the first step toward liberation.

We the people have to hold our leaders accountable for helping us to achieve independence. We have obviously been treated much worse than the invading colonists. If they had a right to declare independence in 1776, how much more do we have a human right to declare our independence after 200 additional years of oppression? The big picture solution is to fight for educational, political, economic and media independence. We have to teach our children to take up this fight and hold our leaders accountable for helping revive our own cultural and social system. Only then will we have justice. Only then can we become free. If our leaders are not helping us to achieve this, then we need to fire them and choose new ones. Nobody's scripture says integrate with the Devil. Everybody's scripture says come out from among them who steal, kill and destroy, who exalt their thrones above God with a unilateralist superiority complex. To want to integrate with the same people who mistreat every generation of black people is pathological. We call this the hostage syndrome.

Hostage negotiations reveal that, if a hostage situation is prolonged, oftentimes the hostage will fall in love with the hostage taker. The hostage will even be defensive of the hostage taker. This is madness. It illustrates the Black American's desire to integrate. We have lost our minds. We have become mentally and emotionally ill, even retarded. The media has given us a dramatic view of this retardation. One movie in particular featured a slave, yet Alex Haley titled it oppositely, "Queen." This is typical of the sordid satire of Hollywood. This mentally and emotionally retarded hostage supposedly fell in love with the hostage taker. We will look at another aspect of Alex Haley's family in the next section. This is also an example of the kind of behavior exemplified in the battered wife syndrome. Europeans kick our behinds and shoot us down anytime they damn well please. Yet we are afraid to leave them because we love them so much. We have been dehumanized for so long that we don't even know how to express human desires.

Compare our plight to the parallel experience of the Palestinians. Our land was stolen. Their land was stolen. That is pretty much where the similarity ends. They refuse to integrate with the people who stole their land and murder them with repressive regularity. We desire to integrate with the people who stole our land and murder us with repressive regularity. They are fighting for their human right to have a place for their children to survive. We are not fighting for our human right to have a place for our children to survive. They denounce the ways of the oppressor. We emulate the ways of the oppressor. We believe it was John Henrik Clarke who said that imitation of the oppressor is not freedom. This parallel was intended to show that Palestinians are behaving like humans with a known right to survive. In contrast, we are behaving like de-humanized slaves with no rights at all except what the slaver chooses to allow. What good is self-determination for a slave? The only thing the slave can determine is that the slaver has all of the answers. We have been beaten down for so long that we believe it is impossible for us to achieve political and economic independence. We will have to overcome this defeatist, slave mentality. Apparently, the Palestinians did not get the memo that says it is impossible to win. We would do well to learn from their struggle.

The sad fact is that most Black Americans don't even want to be free. We prefer to live with our noses up the oppressor's butt while we wait on crumbs to fall from his stolen table of loot. Or we decide to become his same gender sex toy so that we can live the good life. Slavery is definitely not over. In fact, we are more entrenched into perpetual slavery than we have ever been. Each generation becomes more enslaved and less able to free itself than the one before it. We are nearing a dangerous point of no return wherein we remain the lackeys of Eurocentric society until the end of humanity. South Africans are even in a better position than we are in. Palestinians know who they are. South Africans know who they are. We, on the other hand, are mostly clueless. If they decide to put us in ovens, what is going to stop them? Who is going to stop them? It is imperative that we begin to understand the dangers of not being able to say "Never Again." It is extremely dangerous not to have a strategy of keeping these things from happening. Simply having faith in the benevolence of the slaver is foolish and terminally irresponsible. We cannot say "Never Again" because we do not have a political entity with which to defend ourselves.

Our situation is much worse than taxation without representation. We will never be taken seriously and respected by Europeans in the U.S., or anyone else for that matter, unless we have our own political domain and the ability to defend ourselves. Continued subjugation leaves our sons vulnerable of being drafted into the invader's military to protect and to forward white supremacist domination. Vince Rogers has mentioned that we are the only people in the world who fight for someone else's right to rule. The simple solution here is to never join the U.S. military for any reason at any time. Follow the example of strong black men like Muhammad Ali and Malcolm X. If you are a warrior by nature, then fight for your own freedom. Don't fight for the freedom of the oppressor to dominate the globe and destroy the world. This is self-defeating. We are already paying taxes to the oppressor so that he can further oppress us. We are paying taxes so that he can destroy our family all around the Atlantic. We are paying taxes that enable the virus to spread. We are paying taxes to support the death of the planet. We are paying taxes that support the police who still hunt us and brutalize us like it is 1860. Every generation of black people are treated worse than dogs and yet we join his military to secure him even more power to continue to mistreat us. It is unbelievable, embarrassing and dishonorable. When Mohammad Ali was asked why he avoided the draft in Vietnam, he replied, "No Vietcong ever called me nigger."[11] This is a lesson in understanding who we are so that we can know who our enemy is.

The Taliban is not the enemy of our freedom. Iraq is not the enemy of our freedom. Who crushed our movement for freedom in the 1960's and turned it into a movement for integration through civil rights? It was not Arabs. Stand up for independence and you will see who the enemy of our freedom is. The enemy of our freedom is the same entity that we go to fight for when we join the U.S. military. How ridiculous is that? This gives them more power to keep us from ever becoming free. We are teaching our children the societal mores of perpetual slavery. It is no mystery why each generation is worse off. We have some kind of misguided slave love for our children. We teach them to grow up and be good slaves. We do not teach them to grow up and become politically independent and sovereign over their own affairs. We sadly teach them to emulate the oppressor. This is not freedom. It is long past time for us to reverse this condition and change this cycle. It begins with defining our reality outside of a boxed in slave consciousness.

Chapter 6

Prisoners of War

IN this chapter, we will chronologically explain the text box outline of slavery in the U.S. Changing prisoners of war into spiritual slaves was complete by 1865. This process involves disconnecting people from their God-given spirituality and replacing it with the slaver's religion. This is one of the first steps because it makes people easier to dominate and enslave. To reverse this process, we must let go of the slaver's religions and embrace our ancestral spirituality. This would start a process of liberation and healing. The spirituality of our ancestors can liberate both the invader and the prisoner of war. Notice that prior to the spiritual invasion of the Americas, West Africans had been invaded by Christians and Muslims. Before Europeans began taking slaves from West Africa, Muslims were coming all the way across the Sahara desert to enslave them. Too many of us are in denial about Christianity and Islam being slaver's religions and, therefore, anti-liberating. As we remember that liberation is the goal of survival and sustainability, we can transform our current venues of religiosity into centers of spiritual healing through understanding Nature.

The other process, that the text box shows as complete by 1865, is physical slavery. Once the slave is made, you can take the chains off. Remember slavery began in 1865. Prior to this was the making of a slaves from prisoners of war. Do not let them damage your child's psyche by teaching them that an invading, but benevolent European set black people free. We already discussed the solution to physical slavery as full human independence. The fact is we will never have justice until we have our own justice system. To think otherwise shows our inability to recognize the invader's architecture of perpetual injustice. Perpetual slavery obviously includes perpetual injustice. Fighting for justice within this system is futile. It can help to relieve the pain, but it is not a cure for oppression. As we struggle for rights within the system, we must not forget to keep our eyes on our human right to create our own system. We can start by developing autonomous communities wherein we control the policing and the judging. There were no jails here in 1491, so we do have precedent for being able to create harmonious societal structures without jails. Of course, we will not learn about any of this in schools. It does not benefit the oppressor. Jails are part of what he uses to control us and to maintain prisoners of war. According to the 13th amendment, prisons are where they house legal slaves. Since September 11, 2001, they can throw any of us into this legal slavery at any time. All they have to do is label you a terrorist. If we live in our own autonomous communities, this would be much harder for them to do.

Our condition is not unsalvageable. We just need to recognize what the real problems are as opposed to being told what the problems are by the same people who created them. Of course, they often use the mouths of handpicked, sold out black leaders. The solution here is to never listen to any black leader who is not trying to help us become liberated from European domination. Do not listen to leaders who are playing their game of integration because their loyalty is with the white supremacist system. They will sell out millions of black people for personal gain. Listen to those who are creating strategy based on our natural way of doing things, not on the oppressor's way of doing things. In this way we will be implementing methods of recovery from slavery and will begin to learn again how to survive on our own as human beings rather than as de-humanized slaves. Once the making of spiritual and physical slaves was complete in 1865, the next part of the cycle was the making of mental slaves. This involved schooling, which was inaccurately called education. In the late 1800s, they were called normal schools. Of course, what is normal for a predator is not normal for the prey. It becomes clear to us that it will take liberating education to reverse the slave schooling which began just after 1865. Slave schooling or P.O.W. schools are based on the idea that we are already free. Liberation schools are based on the idea that we must acquire the education necessary to exercise our human right to spiritual, physical and mental sovereignty. This is a solution to the problem of mental slavery. No adult or child should be purposely left behind. It is more than just a slogan.

Creating mental slaves was a long process. Although state sponsored schools were slave schools, black folks still found ways to overcome the mental bondage. Even under strong repression, it still took another 100 years for the invading culture to gain sufficient control of our minds to give us the right to vote. This marks the near completion of mental slavery. We became more controlled by information as television became a greater force in our lives. We seem to no longer teach our children to counter repressive domination. *Agents of Repression* by Churchill and Wall should be a staple in our schools. Its content is described by its subtitle, *The FBIs Secret Wars Against the Black Panther Party and the American Indian Movement*. The age of information slavery is when the media dominates our thinking even more than schooling or anything we learned from our parents and elders. Film and music are the main culprits, although print mediums are culpable as well. These mediums are strictly controlled to maintain dominance. The solution is not so simple, since we have become addicted to media even more than drugs. The damage the media has done has been worse than the damage of drugs because media messages appear innocuous. We do not recognize the foreign invasion. This is the same way a virus invades and then we become too weak to fight back. It is a deadly game that is being played on us. Our survival literally depends on us being able to process liberating information.

It is not likely that we will be able to get licensing to spread liberating ideas. Licensing is one method used to control information. A hip hop group named Dead Prez suggested that we simply turn off the radio since they are not going to play anything liberating. The problem is that we are extremely addicted to it. That is like telling a crack head to simply put down his pipe. Because of our strong addiction to slave maintaining media, we are going to need support groups. Media ownership can only help reverse the process of slavery if we are constantly broadcasting or printing liberating messages. Our children are incessantly inundated with White-Supremacist-Christian-Capitalism from the time they wake up in the morning until they go to bed at night. Then their dreams are still confined to the same slave consciousness. If you do not believe me, ask them. Ask them about their dreams and aspirations. You will find that even their dreams remain in the box. The older they get, the more boxed in they become. We have to combat this programming purposefully and constantly. We cannot fight information nukes with information paint balls. As part of the solution, we will have to use the internet to our greatest advantage. For poor people who cannot afford it, all we can say is cancel cable T.V., throw away the cell phone and get internet service.

In order to control our flow of information, we have to get back to having neighborhood meetings. Remember we come from a participatory democracy. It takes longer to get results than it does in a dictatorship or republic; but our survival depends on us being true to who we are, not on seeing how much we can act like a virus by emulating the invader. We have to involve all of our people. We cannot continue to let the masses of our people be sold out by a few hand-picked leaders who have been trained by the oppressor. We must include all families and classes to the best of our ability. We have to organize for liberation and defend against infiltration. We need to discuss what we have learned from the counter-intelligence programs of the 1960s. So far, it seems like the only thing we have learned is to stop fighting for freedom. The completion of information slavery is punctuated by our lack of desire and inability to fight back. Full psychological control is in effect. We are being handled. We are being managed spiritually, mentally and emotionally. This is partly why there was no riot after the Sean Bell verdict in New York.

Our emotions are being managed. We listed New Millennium Slavery as beginning in 1992. That date was used because it was the time of the Rodney King riots. We have entered a new era in which our pain has become so normalized that we seldom fight back. The process is first spiritual, then physical, then mental, then emotional. In this last stage of the process, we no longer possess the motivational emotion to defend ourselves. In this frame of mind, what future do we have besides slavery? This is actually beyond human rights because the anti-Nature creature we call European takes away the right of all living things to defend themselves. The disarmament of Iraq and the destruction of the Black Panther Party for Self Defense are not anomalies. He has even taken away the cow's horns so that she cannot defend herself. All creatures, including humans, are bred, modified, forced or tricked into accepting European domination without the ability to defend themselves. New Millennium Slavery disconnects people from any thoughts and means to liberation. It is intended to last forever, or at least until the end of humanity.

Some of the latest enslaving tricks have been the ideas of sameness and inclusiveness. These modes of thought are programmed into our minds without actually treating us the same or including us. These latest tricks carry the information that has led us from mental slavery into perpetual slavery. The means for this malicious trickery were developed through divisive capitalistic individualism. We were brothers and sisters up until the 1970s. In the New Millennium, we have become profane caricatures of ourselves. We have sold unity for money. We chase fiat dollars so that we can become the mindless, consuming robots that we have been programmed to be. Freedom cannot be bought or given. Freedom must be fought for. These problems result from not understanding who we are. Perpetual slavery is the result of a perpetual identity crisis. Ultimately, the core problem remains that of an identity crisis. For example, if a horse knows he is a horse, you will not be able to get on its back. You must change his identity through enslavement and teach him that he is your carriage. Incidentally, it is said that the oppressor may be willing to do anything to help relieve your pain, except get off of your back. In our case, we may even get a chance to run the oppressor's system, but we will not be allowed to create our own system or a non-oppressive system. What difference does it make who is running the system if it is oppressive? As it has been said in Africa, the colonial powers have not left the continent; they have only changed colors.

In an earlier section, we considered an analogy of the making of a slave dog. It is the same as the horse. As long as he knows he is a dog, he is not going to stay in your yard and eat your dry food. Again, you must change his identity through enslavement and teach him that he is your pet. The same is true for Black Americans. Enslavement is not over because the chains have been taken off; nor is it over because we can come to the table for crumbs and scraps. True to the Malcolm X analogy, the wound does not begin to heal until the identity is restored. Freedom does not become accessible until our identity is restored. If we knew who we were, we would not let Europeans in the U.S. tax us and ride our backs. If we knew who we were, we would not remain in his political domain and eat his edible food-like substances. We borrowed the food description from Michael Pollan. Of course, prisoners of war eat the food that is supplied. One way to begin to break the yoke of slavery is create local food economies to re-gain control of our food production. We recognize no sense of urgency because we do not understand European invasion and the starvation that follows. Solving the problem of our identity crisis has several benefits including the liberation of the Black American family and our ecological environment from the prison of European dominance.

Chapter 7

Name It and Claim It

THE plight of the Black American identity crisis has been similar in some respects to that of South Africans. The Dutch and the English invaded South Africa and stole everything to include their identity. They call themselves South Africans and call the indigenous people Kaffir. Likewise, the English invaded the U.S. and stole everything including our identity. They call themselves Americans and call the indigenous people Niggers or Indians. If it seems like we are claiming that Black Americans are indigenous to the U.S., you are correct. That is exactly what we are trying to convey. This is the part of our identity that we are steered away from and the reason why we never actually understand who we are. We are mostly from the Southeastern part of what is now the U.S. Sure there was a small number of Africans who were brought here. Most were worked to death like machines with a class life of seven years. As far as restoring our identity is concerned, we are the red paint people of the Atlantic Basin. You can dig anywhere in the Southeastern U.S. and you will find artifacts of people who look like us. All of the ideas that we are introducing, we will broaden and treat in greater detail. We just wanted to reiterate that the invader not only steals land, labor and ingenuity, but he also steals the indigenous identity. This is what keeps us from being able to recover from our condition of endless servitude. We are not taught that the foreign invader is an occupier. We learn that he is the rightful tenant of the land as if he bought land that was never for sale.

As part of stealing the identity the invader also steals your name. There are several layers of identity theft. Once we have come beyond the veil of ignorance, we find that there is another veil in place to keep us in the dark. Let's work through some unveiling. The leaders in the U.S. arrogantly refer to their occupied domain as America. Of course, this is a false identity. America is two twin continents that span from northern Alaska to Tierra del Fuego. The U.S. is not America. The U.S. is a sub-section of North America. This kind of labeling from political leaders is a subliminal attempt to claim the entire Western Hemisphere, which brings us to the next layer of deception. Europeans call themselves Westerners. We casually talk about Western science, Western religion and Western society. This only makes sense if Native Americans and West Africans are invisible. Indigenous Americans originated here. Why is Native American culture not considered Western? Western European culture has its roots in Greece, which is not even in the Western Hemisphere. The English came from low Germans. They are not Western either. They may come from the Caucasus Mountains. We do not know. What we do know is that they are not Western. Using the term Western to describe Europeans who invaded the West is another layer of identity theft. In stealing our identity, they seek to take over our existence. Let us be clear about the fact that Western Europeans are not Western. They are European. Westerners include West Africans and Native Americans which make up who we are biologically and culturally. The perception of European invaders of the West as Westerners effectively erases the actual people and culture of the West out of existence.

The Western Hemisphere begins in Mali and in Ghana stretching west to Hawaii. This includes North and South America and the Caribbean islands. We have already explained why Western people are not the current people of Spain, Portugal, England and Ireland. These are not Westerners. These are invaders of the west. Just like a virus tries to claim rightful tenancy in our bodies, Europeans claim to be Western as if the real Americans and West Africans are invisible. This is an important distinction of identity because Black Americans are people of the Atlantic. We are made up of West Africans and Indigenous Americans; therefore, Black Americans are true Westerners, as opposed to invaders of the west. It is suicidal for Indigenous people around the Atlantic to allow European invaders to usurp our Western identity and our land. It furthers the genocidal strategy of perpetual domination. We have to liberate ourselves from the language of the oppressor in order to enter modes of thinking that promote freedom. Correcting these inaccuracies help us to define our own reality in a way that lifts us out of the spooky shadows of invisibility into a more humane existence. Calling the European by name takes away part of his power to deny our survival. Our survival depends on following the power of Mother Nature. She will not steal our identity to erase our independent existence. She will help us understand who we are and help us to survive.

Since we have been explaining who the real Americans are and who they are not, it is necessary to also explain the name "America" itself. We have been taught that America was named by a German fellow who gave it this name after a so-called explorer named Amerigo Vespucci. Once again, if you blindly believe the mis-informative history that the invaders craftily conjure up, then you will never find the information necessary for liberation. This fictionalized story of the naming of America is yet another layer of deception which pretends again that the indigenous people are invisible. America is a Mayan word indigenous to Mexico. One good resource on this information is *Fulcrums of Change* by Jan Carew which we quoted from earlier. The name 'America' is associated with strong winds such as those of hurricanes. The origin of this language is near the Yucatan peninsula which is known to be cyclically pounded by hurricanes. Incidentally, Mexico and hurricane are also indigenous words. The strong wind is similar to the breath that God breathed into Adam in the Torah and Bible. The Godliness of the wind and water mix complete with the circular motion and still center gives rise to thoughts of heaven and thus paradise. The essential energy in the word 'America' has spawned at least a book and a movie both with the title, Conquest of Paradise. America has always been seen as paradise. This is why the Moors came here; and this is why Columbus came as well.

The Moors brought Columbus to America. This Italian man opened the door for the virus to spread in America. The nerve center of this spreading virus is not surprisingly named the District of Columbia. Is this political entity a friend or foe? What does hundreds of years of data show? As Dr. White used to jokingly say, a leopard does not change his spots. We are in need of protection from the same harbingers of death that have proliferated in the U.S. for more than 200 years. We have shown this viral infection as the cause of the Black American identity crisis. The stealing of our identity coincided with the stealing of our farms, homes and freedom. Let us not continue to be vague about who the enemy of our freedom is. We obviously have misunderstood the fundamental definition of freedom since we are still joining the fight for the freedom of Europeans in the U.S. to kill whomever they want whenever they want. This is what they call freedom. Fighting for the U.S. is not fighting for **OUR** freedom. This is fighting for the freedom of white supremacists to mercilessly dominate everyone else. As we begin to define and name things for ourselves, misinformation is corrected. The possibilities of freedom for black people become clear. Toward further healing of the viral infection which has caused our identity crisis, let's look at an outline of the immune system.

Chapter 8

Four Steps of the Immune System

If we want to be a healthy people again, we need to consider Mother Nature's model of health. Our God-given model of health and harmony can be found inside of ourselves as our immune system. In order to return to health, we must follow the same path that we learn from our immune system. The first step is to recognize that which is foreign. This is why the first section of this book has been dedicated to recognizing foreign invasion. We have tried to elucidate some things about ourselves by learning about that which is foreign. In so doing, we hope to have brought to light some of the issues that are enemies of health. Remember all of our cells have cell markers, which are identifiers. As long as we are nourished and foreign material is kept out, we will generally be healthy. We cannot allow ourselves to be inundated daily with toxic foreign material and still expect to be healthy. We have to remain true to our identity so that we can recognize that which is foreign. We must be able to clearly identify who we are; otherwise we will not be able to determine what is out of place or what does not belong. Stated differently, knowledge of self should clarify what is non-self.

Once the body's defenses have been breached and we have recognized foreign invasion, the second step is to neutralize the effect of the foreign material to keep it from multiplying. The invader designed counterintelligence programs to perpetuate invasion. We have to design counter-slavery strategies, like vigilant lymphocytes, to neutralize the effects of the invasion. This will keep slavery from multiplying. Since the invasion is constant, the neutralization methods must also be organized and constantly implemented. This means that we must deprogram our children every day. We cannot combat subliminal messages everyday with a meeting once a week. After we have neutralized the effect of foreign invasion, the third step is to expel the foreign material. It is necessary to eliminate all of the foreign material so that it can no longer harm the body. While it is true that the body can live in relative health with a minimal amount of foreign substance, it is best to eliminate all foreign matter that can possibly be expelled. Then it is necessary to have a plan to eliminate the remaining sickness at the earliest opportunity. Once we have eliminated all possible foreign material, then our final task is to remember the foreign invasion to keep it from ever happening again.

The nature of the invasion and the nature of the solution must be ritualistically observed in order to keep the virus from infecting future generations. The stories must be re-told to every generation as part of our historical and religious heritage. Once we have followed God's model of health given to us in our immune system, then we can finally say "Never Again." Specifically, we can put spiritual, mental, physical and emotional measures in place to keep from ever being invaded by Europeans again. Using this model requires that we remove everything European from our lives including all Eurocentric thought. Some might argue that we have some European blood, so Europeans are not entirely foreign to us. Our response is that the part of the virus that you allow to remain will likely grow to haunt your progenitors. Just because you have some virus in you does not mean that you should allow it to linger. We have tried that foolishness before. Historical precedent shows us that the virus will mutate if allowed to remain. It will change names or change forms, become unrecognizable and continue to destroy. Slavery is one case in point. If we are to live healthful lives, then we must get the virus out. To make this process of deprogramming simple and easy to implement, we will reduce it to four words that we can easily recall: Recognize, Neutralize, Expel and Remember.

When we were young children, we were programmed with an old adage that says if you can't beat them, join them. Cartoons are one method used to build this framework in a child's mind. It is intended to inhibit any thoughts of resistance as a pre-emptive counter insurgency strategy. If we stay focused on Mother Nature and how our immune system heals the body, we will be much less vulnerable to the psychological warfare that defeats us even before we get started to fight for the survival of our children. If you cannot beat a virus, you do not join the virus. If you integrate with the virus, then you become a virus as well. Our behavioral changes since integration in the 1970s make this obvious. As we have advanced in the workplace, the institutional virus uses us for an even greater degree of exploitation. With each generation, we become more complicit with our own destruction. Harmony, health and balance depend on us defending ourselves and our ecology from viral invasion.

Fortunately, methods of defense are creatively limitless, since blacks in the U.S. are almost defenseless. Our situation is significantly different from that of Africans who have their own nations and militaries. The problem that we must solve is not Pan African. The best thing that we can do for ourselves and Africa is to become a free nation right here in this land. Without the meddling of the European Diaspora, Africa can heal herself. What is important for us to realize is that we are not the same as Europeans, but we are not the same as Africans either. If we are going to spend time marching in Washington, we should insist that the Great Satan let our people go. We are not alluding to a back to Africa movement. We are saying let freedom ring right here in the land of our blood, sweat and tears.

We are writing about liberating ourselves from America's foreign invading virus, which is Europeans. This historical fact and current reality has infected people all over the world. The deadly infection is most pressing at the current time in Afghanistan and Iraq. The empirical evidence makes it clear who the virus is. We wish it were as simple as wanting to dominate the human family as a self-proclaimed superior. This problem of virus behavior extends to all living things. It doesn't matter what rhetoric is used in defense, but the behavior of the European Diaspora is anti-life. It doesn't just affect the human family. It affects Mother Earth and all of her children. Europeans are out of control and are destroying the whole world, especially from the U.S. They did not listen in 1492 when they were told they were destroying the world by the Taino. Now, their very late environmental science makes this issue undeniable. Indigenous Americans and other people in the world had already figured out that you cannot live against Mother Nature and survive for very long. Our focus in this writing is on the emancipation of our full human potential. Not only is independence necessary to reach this goal, but joining forces with Mother Nature is also part of the plan to ensure sustainability. We strongly oppose the destruction and dominance of the foreign, invading European. The more we understand who we are, the better we will be able to recognize non-self. As our identity is further revealed, we will be able to resist the attack of viruses and become a healthy people. Foreign invasion is the cause of our identity crisis. In order to protect ourselves, our children and our Earth, we have to Recognize, Neutralize, Expel and Remember foreign invasion.

Part 2

Incomplete Identity

"We must understand who we are, where we are and what is going on."

Dr. William White

Chapter 9

Afrocentrism

BUILDING on Dr. White's quote that starts this section, the question of who we are has largely to do with the biogenetic self. Where we are has to do with the cultural self. What is going on has to do with the societal self. We will start this section off with concerns about who we are biologically. One of the first questions Dr. White would ask people when they gravitated to his teachings is, "who are you?" So far in this book, we have mainly been sharing information about who we have become politically. We explained European invasion as the cause of our identity crisis. This is how we came to such an extreme misunderstanding about who we are. Now, we would like to turn our attention to some issues relating to who we are ethnically and ecologically. To contribute to a more meaningful discussion of our knowledge of self, we will combine an inner, intuitive understanding with the theoretical logic of history.

Who we are at the present time is inextricably connected to our origins, since we are made up of all those who lived before us in our ethno-cultural ancestry. Therefore, the truth of who we are remains inside of us…inside of us individually and inside of our interrelations. The introspective portion of the journey is more important than usual because European invasion has cut us off from much of the memory of our past. Proper education is supposed to bring out who we are. However, the systemic mis-education process does not include any introspective guidance or practice. As a result, we do not take advantage of our moments of solitude that could be used to expand our intellect through meditation. We cannot reach an adequate understanding of our past through Western European intellectualism. Our ancestry is both external and internal. The internal part is off limits to the invader. In order to overcome historical oppression, we will have to develop that part of our historical consciousness that the aggressor cannot invade and control.

As we consider our own origins and the origins of others in the human family, it is interesting to note one way that science is being used to help us connect with our identity. Recently the invader has been going around the world with his DNA studies in an attempt to confirm for the world that he and his knowledge are superior. We are naturally suspicious of this activity. We will elaborate on this after analyzing the paradigm developed from previous scientific studies. For quite some time Eurocentric science has held the position that human beings or Homo sapiens first emerged in East Africa. Since the application of Eurocentric knowledge is destroying the planet at an alarming pace, we should suspect that there may be some fundamental flaws with what they think is scientific and technologically advanced. Eurocentric science is based on the assumption that they are superior. The results always further the cause of white supremacy. Otherwise, the results are not well publicized. The information is much less accessible if it is honest and independent or does not support global domination. The problem of restoring our identity is further complicated by academic entrenchment. For example, Charles Darwin's theory of evolution is popularly applied to linear approaches that attempt to explain our origins.

Around 1973, Dr. Donald Johanson found some very old leg bones in Ethiopia of a female subsequently named Lucy. It was reported that 40% of a skeleton was complete. It has been argued that parts of the skeleton were found up to a mile away. This is relevant to the claims of Lucy being half-hominid because the knees were not found near the body. Lucy is considered a hominid mainly because of her legs. If parts of her legs are found in other places, how do we know they are her legs? We cannot rule out a fitting of the bones to our pre-conceived notions of her being a biped. This has been an academic pillar of support for Darwin's theory of evolution. Another pillar in support of linear evolution from Africa is the footprints found by Dr. Mary Leakey around 1978. She found these footprints in Tanzania and postulated that they were produced from a biped who may be an ancestor of humans. As with the bones of Lucy, the dating is 3-4 million years ago. Neither of these finds provides us with a missing link to the origin of the human family. While both of these half-ape creatures are extinct, we are left with some groundwork for where Europeans are searching for their origins and how they are approaching the problem. There is no particular reason why we should follow this direction other than universities are set up based on the linear evolution paradigm which, for humans, is assumed to begin in Africa. Darwin's theory is the broad evolutionary paradigm. Johanson and Leakey support this paradigm with old bones found in Africa. The conclusion that we may be unfamiliar with is that the old bones found in Africa are not Hominids. The research follows a linear, mathematical process which does not reflect the dynamic, creative process of life on Mother Earth.

We propose that humans may not have a linear origin on a flat Earth. Rather, we may have multiple origins on a sphere. Darwin's evolution and the paradigm that was built around it are not consistent with the dynamic process of Mother Earth giving birth to new entities. The energy from within the Earth flows to the surface in multiple places at the same time. Old bones are found all over the world. More recent findings are ignored or suppressed because they do not fit the body of knowledge that people have been effectively programmed and subdued with. The academic community only accepts data that is biased towards a singular linear origin for all humans. Just because Johanson has possibly found the oldest part Hominid bones to date does not mean that we have identified the physical beginning of humanity. Have we searched the whole world? Have we considered other ancient places that do not fit the white supremacist paradigm? What changed Lucy's children into humans? Who was her husband? Did these same conditions exist elsewhere around the equator? Must humans be reduced to only one origin to spread out in linear fashion around the globe? Does this provide us with a basis for explaining Asian eyes, European hind parts or Hawaiian complexion? None of these questions are answered by building on the scientific foundation of Darwin, Johanson and Leakey.

Lucy is actually meaningless as an explanation of human origins. She was not even a human. She is not a missing link. All we can say is that Dr. Johanson found some old bones. The general framework of the Lucy origin maintains the image of black inferiority. Europeans know that they are the youngest bipeds on the planet. In order to use this information to their advantage, they lead us to believe that they are the most evolved and therefore superior. They want us to believe that Africans, and thus black people, are old and primitive while Europeans are more evolved and more advanced. This is one of the main reasons Eurocentric science promotes the idea of

African human origins. The other main reason has to do with the invasion of the Americas. Unfortunately, we get so caught up blindly believing in Eurocentric science that we lose sight of the big picture. This is an example of what was discussed previously about our critical analysis remaining inside the box. Black Americans really do not examine this body of Eurocentric scholarship with any insightful scrutiny because Lucy gives us something African to hold on to. We reach an emotional conclusion rather than using our non-Eurocentric intellect to develop a historical reality of our own through critical inquiry.

The invader has to lock us into being African in order to keep control of the U.S. By playing his tricks of origin on us, he takes our attention away from what is going on here and takes us into a hypnotic trance focused completely on Africa. Although, it is quite an undertaking, we will try to explain how this fits into the invader's historical paradigm and therefore, perpetuates our inferiority complex and our demise. We are not going to mince words here. We are saying that Afrocentrism is an indoctrinated view of the world for us. It is not a complete and relevant identity for Black Americans. If the movie Roots was a true story, it never would have been a part of mainstream media. If we look back at the quote that began the book, it will give us some insight as to how we are being misled. The oppressor will not tell us the truth about our identity. He must create and maintain an identity crisis. When he tells us that we are African and that he brought us here, we should know right away that he is lying. Remember, if he lets the horse know he is a horse, he will not be able to ride him anymore. Once the dog knows he is a dog, he will not stay in the yard; and he will not come back for mass produced food or table scrap welfare.

We believe it was John Henrik Clarke who said the oppressor cannot afford to educate us. Otherwise, he would not be able to oppress us any longer. This is essentially the same thing that Dr. White was trying to convey except that it is more generalized. The irony here is that John Henrik Clarke was Afrocentric. Knowing that the oppressor cannot afford to educate us makes us question the whole department of African American Studies. We are declaring that if African American Studies were useful and liberating, it would not be available at U.S. universities, especially not at institutions that are owned and/or controlled by invading Europeans. These studies are accepted at many universities precisely because they are misleading, mis-educating and perpetuate an incomplete identity for Black Americans. We wear our African medallions and T-shirts. We throw our fists in the air and proclaim our pride in being African as we fight for civil rights and integrate with the oppressor. We never even notice that what we have learned is anti-liberating. Instead of becoming free, we became further entrenched into the same system that abuses us and denies our freedom.

Forcing us further and further away from our own culture and using continuous misinformation tactics have created a veil of ignorance that makes Afrocentric teachings ineffective. We have been given false hopes to hang on to and propped up with foreign self esteem. For example, we were told we came from kings and queens which locks us into class stratification and inequitable capitalism. We were not told the truth that we came from non-hierarchal people who lived in a classless society. According to an article from the political primate (Oct. '07), these are some of the same differences that exist between chimpanzees and orangutans. This evidence from the natural world lends credence to other teachings of Dr. White. He taught that Europeans came from a different branch of the Earth tree. Europeans are hierarchal and hyper-aggressive like the chimpanzee. Indigenous Americans, to include Black Americans, are non-hierarchal without imperial aspirations like the orangutan. It was shown in Part 1 that we are different animals with different natures. We are now suggesting that we have different origins. We are not saying that Europeans come from chimps while Black Americans come from orangutans. We are only saying that this exemplifies our origins and our contemporary behavior. Since Africa is home to several different races of black people, we are limiting this discussion to the small number of Africans in the amalgam of Black Americans.

An honest examination of the African slave trade into the U.S. reveals farmers and pastoral people in our history. The African side of us is not made up of urban kings and queens. The urban pyramid building side of us is from America. We do not need to go anywhere to raise our self-esteem or to make a connection with the land and cosmos. We just need to come out of the supremacist side of the box noted by hierarchal rule. Following the Afrocentric path, we are also told that we come from warriors. I guess that makes us feel macho; but machismo will not liberate us. This is linked to ego issues, not necessarily defense. It does not promote a healthy mentality. Being told that we came from warriors keeps us locked into a box of violence, still in a path of emulation. Of course, most of our violence is black on black and, therefore, never helps to solve the problem of liberation. Defense is more psychological than anything else. If we can learn to defend our minds, much of the physical battle would be thwarted. We do not come from a violent warrior people on either side of the Atlantic. If this was the case, we never would have been enslaved. We are still trying to match European development which includes their warmongering. We never seem to be able to get away from emulating the oppressor which is why we are building on an indigenous perspective that is outside of the box.

The Africans brought to the U.S. did not have the latest technological weapons because they did not need them. They were relatively peaceful people. Our ancestors on the West side of the Atlantic also had no need for elaborate weapons. With that said, it was not weaponry or great warrior aggression that enabled the invader to establish himself with slaves in the U.S. It was his filthy ways that caused the indigenous immune system to give way. We did not become slaves because we were inferior fighters. So, we do not need to pump up our self esteem by teaching our children that we come from warriors. Tell the children the truth. We come from peaceful, non-confrontational people who are fun loving by nature. Following this peaceful state of mind, we solved many of our disputes through ball games as opposed to wars. Compare the 800,000 dead in the African country of Rwanda with our own experience. You could put an automatic weapon in the hand of every aggressive black male in the U.S. Regardless of the conditions we would not kill each other like that. We are not making any judgment on the people of Rwanda. We use this extreme example to help jar our minds into understanding that Africa alone does not capture the full essence of who we are. We are a unique Black American people. We need to understand our Southern Atlantic heritage so that we can finally move beyond a slave mentality into a liberated understanding of who we are.

We should have noticed that the mis-educator encourages us to unify with Africans but discourages us from unifying with each other. Do we not see how we are being played? We cannot actually unify with Africa until we have unified with each other. We can send our few dollars to Africa. Then the European virus can cancel out any benefit from those funds because he still has a stranglehold on both sides of the Atlantic. As mentioned previously, the best thing we can do for ourselves and for Africa is to become politically independent right here. As our identity is restored, we accomplish this. Then Europeans in the U.S. and abroad will not have the wherewithal to maintain a stranglehold on Africa. She will be able to heal herself. Africa doesn't need our paternalistic and emotional sympathy that are useless in solving the core problems that exist on the continent. With our own political entity and defense system, we could have sent troops to Rwanda to stop the genocide while urging a diplomatic and peaceful solution. Since we are still slaves, all we could do was beg the slaver to send troops and lamentably accept the genocide when he refused. If we would fight for our own nation, we could also help stop the genocide in Darfur. We remain powerless simply because we refuse to think in terms of liberation. We refuse to think outside of the box. We refuse to think outside of the Eurocentric creature comforts that have made us apathetic to independent progress. Be advised that oversized homes and luxury cars today will likely ensure starvation and incurable diseases in the future. For now, these things have successfully taken away any motivation to fight for freedom.

One of the more popular destinations in Africa for Black Americans has become South Africa. It is en vogue to go to South Africa. Universities offer study abroad programs there. Even Oprah started a school there. It is good press to be seen as involved in the development of newly freed South Africa. Just as we think we are free in the U.S. because we stood for freedom; we also think South Africa is free because we stood against apartheid. The sacrifices and struggles are commendable, but we are still not free. The shuffling of Black Americans to South Africa is playing into the hands of the controlling elite who are developing U.S. style oppression for the future of this nation. The same methods used to perpetuated slavery in the U.S. will also perpetuate slavery in South Africa. Consider the following part of the script. Freedom fighter Nelson Mandela was a political prisoner in South Africa for 27 years. Freedom fighter Geronimo Pratt was a political prisoner in the U.S. for 27 years. When Mandela was released, they paraded him all around the U.S. with a full scale publicity blitz. This made him a hero and a household name. He was even put on a T-shirt with Malcolm and Martin, even though he is not Black American and has never fought for our freedom. He was used in our Afrocentric teachings.

In sharp contradistinction, there is the case of Geronimo Pratt. Eventually, Johnnie Cochran was able to get him out of jail. He is Black American. He fought for the U.S. in Vietnam and he fought for the oppressed in the Black Panther Party for Self Defense. Upon his release, there was no parade, no publicity and no attempt by the establishment to make him a hero. He did not get a T-shirt with Malcolm and Martin. Are we supposed to believe this is because his name did not start with an "M?" It has been said many times that the white media chooses our heroes. The difficult thing to understand is why we continue to let it happen. Obviously, they made Mandela our hero because he can do absolutely nothing for us. This is the game. This is a technique used over and over again. Whenever we begin to get vociferous with our complaints, the oppressor placates our contentions with a useless pacifier. This buys him time and he continues with the strategy M.L.K. referred to as the "…tranquilizing drug of gradualism."[12] In other words, his answer to apartheid was to parade Mandela around to give us the illusion that the battle had been won. They are using the same strategies on South Africa that they used in the U.S. Why shouldn't they? These perpetual slavery strategies are extremely profitable for them in the U.S. Recall that progress for the people doesn't truly begin until the wound of slavery begins to heal. The wound will not heal while it is infected with a virus.

It is the invading virus who silenced Geronimo Pratt as part of the information slavery that we discussed in the previous section. They do not want us to know who he is because it might help us understand who we are. Most importantly, they do not want us to be aware of anyone who could possibly muster a resurgence of the Panther Party. The resurgence of this organization is also related to the untimely death of Kalid Muhammad. Pratt's first name is additionally a major problem for the establishment which is a definite breach of information slavery. We will explain this further in the following pages. Establishing a sympathetic relationship with South Africa is part of the Eurocentric programming. To the contrary, recognizing our relationship with Geronimo Pratt is taboo. (For the record and out of respect to him, we would like to mention that to the best of our knowledge, he has taken on the name Geronimo ji Jaga.) Since we explained 1865 as the beginning of slavery in the U.S., this should help us understand what is going on in South Africa. It should be obvious that the oppressor wants them to desire to be like us, perpetual slaves. If we want to be an example to South Africans, let's control the information that our children receive and become liberated in the U.S.

What difference does it make if a black man is running the system if it is the same system the invading Europeans left in place? The result will be the same. The foreign invader can promise black leaders the stolen wealth and riches of the Devil. So, what incentive do they have to side with the masses of oppressed people who have been taught to be divisive and apathetic anyway? These are the same tactics used in the U.S. We seem to think our going to South Africa connects us with our ancestors. These emotionally charged travels actually benefit the slaver by helping him to perpetuate slavery on both sides of the Atlantic. It helps Europeans in South Africa keep the indigenous people in a box where they are fully subjugated and controlled while under the impression that they are free. This is a game they play all over the world. The game is to close all doors to liberation. This includes eradicating the thought of liberation, particularly for Black Americans because Europeans are trying to dominate the globe from Washington D.C. This is accomplished by confining our definition of freedom to whatever they want it to be. We are confined to the framework of perpetual slavery with an illusion of freedom. Afrocentrism is part of that dominating framework. Let us see how one of our favorite leaders fared with an Afrocentric mindset and Pan African aspirations.

We have a lot of love for Marcus Garvey and his plans of empowerment through sovereignty. We essentially share many of his ideas. Hindsight enables us to see, however, that Liberia and the back to Africa movement was a failure in terms of liberating the masses of Black Americans. Maybe Jamaican born Marcus Garvey was completely African, but that does not mean that we are. A few elitists and liberation minded people were encouraged to move to Liberia in order to keep them from infecting others of us with a spirit of freedom. Liberia, however, was not a sovereign victory for Black Americans. The establishment of Liberia was used to squash the sovereignty movement of blacks in the U.S. This demonstrates the familiar strategy of giving us something that we cannot use. Our struggles are co-opted and changed to benefit the slaver. Meanwhile, we end up in a worse predicament than we were before the struggle began. Allow us to share another insightful anecdote. W.E.B. Dubois' grandfather was a prisoner of war (during the making of slaves). He was a master carpenter. Because of his great skill, his family lived well as long as he was owned by a slaver. Later, W.E.B. Dubois' father also became a master carpenter with exceptional skills. Unfortunately for him, the Civil War had ended. He was no longer considered property of the invader. For this reason, the same clientele who employed his father would not give him the work. He was not able to provide as well for his family as his father had even though slavery had supposedly ended.

Because the slaver remains in control, whenever things are supposed to get better, they tend to get much better for the slaver but only marginally better for the slave. The slaver was in full control in 1860 and he was still in full control in 1865. He was in control during Marcus Garvey's lifetime and he is still in control in 2009. Freedom in the U.S. has never included black people. Changes occur, but they only benefit the invader and a few hand-picked Negroes. Consequently, we never actually achieve freedom, which is spiritual, political, economic and emotional independence. Afrocentrism is one of those tricks used as a placebo to impotently fill our desire to come to terms with our identity. We do not want to overlook the fact that the back to Africa strategy was tried more than once. The first attempt was the establishment of Freetown in Sierra Leone. It was not any more successful at liberating the masses of Black Americans than Liberia was. But that may not have been the goal of Freetown. Afrocentric thinking has its merits that have been penned elsewhere. This critique exposes that it has not been respectful to Indigenous Americans nor has it been liberating for Africans brought to the U.S. We certainly need to unify against our common enemy; but unity begins at home. For example, Cuba did not have to unify with Africa to become free. We do not have to unify more than 800 million people in the African Diaspora to liberate the 40 million blacks in the U.S.

Chapter 10

Pan-Africanism and Other Connections

TOWARD developing a liberating foundation for Black Americans, we will expose the logic of the African Diaspora. By definition, the Diaspora has to do with ancestral homeland. Using this definition, the African Diaspora has to include everyone who has ancestors from Africa. We should immediately see the problem with the logic given other beliefs we have accepted. If all humans come from Africa, then the African Diaspora would include everyone in the world. We are taught that Africa is the ancestral homeland of all people and make it synonymous with Earth by calling Africa the Motherland. Following this logic, the term African Diaspora includes everyone and, therefore, identifies no one. What we are left with are the connotations associated with the term. One such view involves the slave trade. This covers Africans taken into Europe, the Middle East and the Americas. More practically, the term in the U.S. is applied to African descendants in the Americas. This gives us a starting date of about 1502 for the Diaspora in the Caribbean. For the U.S., our beginning is taught as 1619. In this view of the world, it is unclear as to whether the Moors are absorbed into the indigenous population or considered part of the African Diaspora. The Moors, of course, are the Africans who came to the Americas before Columbus.

Our general usage of the term, African Diaspora, makes it synonymous with blackness. Sometimes it is extended to include everyone in the world who is dark skinned. In this case it totally disrespects the indigenous heritage of people from India, Australia, the South Pacific, the Americas, and anywhere else there are black people who are not African. The idea that all black people are African demonstrates a significantly flawed understanding of

Mother Nature and Mother Earth. We need to be honest about our scholarship. We did not learn this from the Mother. We learned this from European invaders. Of course, Africans will confirm it. Everyone thinks their own people are the original people. Indigenous Americans also think they are the original people. We never considered the possibility of Africans being of an American Diaspora. We offer this opposite idea as an alternative because we have found that it brings us closer to the truth that is capable of liberating us. Civilization is actually older in the Americas than it is in Africa. As far as a liberating identity is concerned, we do not need an emotional connection to a foreign land. We need a real connection to the land beneath our feet.

Worldwide Pan-Africanism is not liberating for Black Americans because it does not provide a truthful or useful basis for solving the problem of our identity crisis. With this view of the world, we would have to claim someone else's land to have a place for our children. As long as we focus on believing what the slaver told us (that he brought us from Africa), then we will never have any real stake in the land of our forebears from the Southeastern U.S. The jailing and killing of our freedom fighters of the 1960s seems to have caused us to be complacent on land dominated by the invader as we fight for civil rights. Recall that there were at least two main fronts of fighting. There were those fighting for civil rights; but there were also those fighting for land-based political sovereignty. For example, Dr. Mack Jones pointed out the liberation struggle of the Republic of New Africa. From the name of this organization and the information we found on its website, we find it to be incomplete. But, we do want to build on the foundation that was laid in an attempt to solve the land problem and identity problem together. We appreciated the Republic of New Africa website's discussion of the successful slave revolt of 1562 in South Carolina. It was mentioned that the Africans were helped by the Native Americans against a common enemy. Interestingly, we are taught that the first Africans were brought in 1619. The story of 1562 helps us to get our thinking outside of the box.

One problem with the geography of the Republic of New Africa (RNA) in the Southeastern U.S. is that it does not recognize the culture of the Indigenous people. These include the Cherokee, Creek, Chickasaw, Yamassee, Natchez, Choctaw and Ouachita, to name some of the better known families. Dr. White taught that Mother Nature favors the home team. One example is of the Moors who were in Spain for 700 years. Eventually, the Spanish got it back. Likewise, Europeans will not be able to stay in America forever. But we do have to fight with Mother America to defend ourselves of the invading virus. A sustainable mind set includes understanding where we are. This is not New Africa as if the future of the Southeast should be a satellite of Africa. Imposing an African mentality in America perpetuates some of the same problems as European invasion. It maintains elements of a colonial mentality. We are also uneasy about a transition from one Republic to another particularly when its roots are foreign. Liberia was supposedly set up for those who want go to Africa. This is not Africa. America has a spirit and a body of her own. While we agree with the expectations and creed of RNA, we cannot ignore the Indigenous people, culture and land in a process of liberation. Unlike the misleading history of the Buffalo soldiers, we suggest that we are children of this land rather than foreign invaders, like Europeans. We certainly have roots in the Southeast, but we argue that we have seeds here too. Knowledge of our Southeastern U.S. identity strengthens our connection with each other and with the land that we need to survive.

NCOBRA has also come to our attention as another organization that promotes our independence in this land. We respect that we need to fight on all fronts. We do not expect much to come of reparations, however. From an Indigenous American perspective, it becomes clear that the invader never kept any treaties. Consequently, Dr. White insisted that we be mindful in our planning that the invader always cheats. For this reason, we recognize that reparations are likely to be a vulnerable source of trickery. Recall the fight against the rebel flag on top of the capitol building in South Carolina. The concession was to take it off of the top of the building, but they put it in front of the building. This is the way the trickster deals. It is likely that any fight for reparations will be reduced to fiat money at a strategic time when the money will be of little value. Reparations in land are seen as requesting land of the oppressor toward repairing the damage of Black Americans. We hold the position that it is not his land to give. Correcting our identity crisis will improve our ability to demand our land as we build on the fight of the previous generation. While we may differ with the perspective and strategy of other Nationalist organizations, we stand unified with them. We are always vigilant of falling prey to divide and conquer. Regardless of our critique, we stand unified with all of the people and organizations that we have mentioned in this book. We have only attempted to point out alternative ways of looking at our problems so that we can devise sustainable solutions. In order to have a future independent of domination, we will have to flood Nationalist organizations with energy and resources as we develop them through dialogue. Civil Rights help to relive the pain; but it takes independence to cure the illnesses of injustice, inequality and oppression.

We have half a millennium of clearly relevant data that substantiates our human right to independence. We have all the necessary nation building skills to be completely self-reliant. We have ingenuity unmatched anywhere in the world, not even on the continent of Africa. There is an entire encyclopedia of Black American inventions that the modern world uses. That does not even include those that were stolen by the invader. We have become world leaders in spite of oppression. Even in a downtrodden state of mind, we resonate with the tone of harmony for the whole world. The world moves to Black American rhythms, not the rhythms of Africa. The world moves to the beat of our drum, which for better or worse, is imitated all over the world. African music is not. We do not even listen to African music and we are supposed to have come from there. The effect of Black American liberation can easily become the shot heard around the world to fan the flames of liberation struggles internationally. This is why incessant repression is used against us. As a responsibility of our generation, we must not cease fighting for freedom. We want to build on rather than abandon the freedom struggles from previous generations. We want to build not only on our fight for national land, but also build on a more complete view of our national identity.

Regardless of what happens in Africa, the masses of our people still have to survive here. Otherwise, we are still subjected to some other country's sovereignty. If we move to Ghana, for example, then we are subject to the sovereignty of Ghana. It is still not our own. We want our own just like our cousins in the Caribbean. Liberia does not solve this problem. We have been reluctant to think in terms of claiming the fruits of our labor because of the crafty spin doctors. They teach us that the foreign invader is an American while the indigenous black people are foreigners. We are encouraged to use a foreign name such as African American or just African. Internalized in our minds, the invader becomes the rightful and normal tenant while we become the foreigner. Just as the predator plasters us onto the prime time news as if we are the predators, he also programs us to believe that we are the foreigners. Hopefully, we can see how damaging this is to our psyche, our identity and our ability to survive. Why should we be the ones to leave? We are not the ones who invaded, notwithstanding the trickery involved with the Buffalo Soldiers. We are not the perpetrators, nor the beneficiaries of Manifest Destiny, which is a euphemism for genocide.

We are not suggesting that there were no Africans brought here. We only mean to say that there were less than half a million brought to the U.S. during the entire transatlantic slavery period. Most of those were worked to death. If they managed to live and have children, those children were often born of an indigenous woman. When we put the pieces together, we find that we are of indigenous heritage and rightful inheritors of this land. This is why the establishment wants us to focus on Africa. Studying about Africa is great if you plan to move to Africa. It is of little to no use for the masses of our people who will remain here. This is why we repeat that Afrocentrism is not liberating and Pan Africanism is equally misleading. Oppositely, we need to study as much as we can about indigenous America. Many free Africans survived here by learning indigenous culture. If we have been seeking truth for some time, then surely we have observed that truth is nearly opposite the information that is put out by mainstream media. For example, if they say the U.S. is the home of the free, then it is more likely to be the home of slaves. It is a more efficient use of time, at least, to start our research with the opposite of mainstream. They say we are from the East. If we want to know the truth and we understand the games they play, then we should start our research in the West to find the origins of our biological and cultural selves. Invading Europeans have been known to manipulate or falsely represent the facts of Nature in order to advance the viral infection of white supremacy. As we continue our research, we must keep in mind that these tricksters perpetuate campaigns of misinformation on both sides of the Atlantic.

Consider a different paradigm altogether. We know that we come from Mother Earth. Let us give some thought to how that might occur. In looking for human origins, it should be useful to discuss the origin of life on Earth, especially if our world view includes evolution. We note that evolution and creationism are not necessarily opposing ideas. A new creation can come from an existing structure and be perceived as evolution. In terms of evolution and creation, we find that bacteria are the first children of Mother Earth. At some time in the distant past, bacteria began to show up in the hot pools of water. These bacteria began to show up all over the planet where supporting conditions existed. All bacteria did not start from one bacterium named Lucy and spread in linear fashion around the surface of the Mother. Sure, they multiplied and spread. The point is that they spread from multiple sources. We are suggesting that the origins of life on Earth are multiple and dynamic rather than linear and deterministic. Mother Earth is quite capable of giving birth to more than one kind, even simultaneously. One plausible explanation for this is that the optimal mix of chemicals and conditions existed in more than one place on the planet when it became time for the seeds of life to germinate. When we are thinking of origins, we have to keep in mind that Earth energy originates within the sphere and lifts to multiple points on the surface. It does not originate on the surface and then proceed in linear fashion around the surface.

One of the reasons we find it difficult to gain a clear understanding of origins is that television and educational mediums have programmed us to be narrowly focused on the concept of roots. Of course, this keeps us stuck in the middle of the story without a firm grasp on the beginning. Roots are not the beginning. The seed is a starting point. With this in mind, we cannot be confused about trick questions like, "which comes first, the chicken or the egg?" Creationism, particularly from the Torah and Bible, is what initiated this confusion in the U.S. If we know that Mother Nature teaches us the seed is the beginning, then we also know it is not possible to start off with an adult chicken, or a chicken and rooster for that matter. The egg has to come first in the real world. A misinformed or politically charged priest may write down something that we believe in, like the chicken comes first; but that does not change the reality that a chicken comes from an egg. Recognize that belief and truth can be two vastly different things. Truth is liberating. Belief is confining. The truth to discover in this case is where the seeds come from, or where the eggs come from. If everything else on this planet evolved from bacteria, then where did the bacteria come from? We know that human females are born with eggs and also with a womb from which they give birth to fertilized eggs. Even with the sea horse, the eggs come from the Mother. It stands to reason then that Mother Earth must have seeds/eggs and also have a womb. Incidentally, some human females are born with more than one womb. It should be obvious that Mother Earth has more than one womb since she can and does give birth simultaneously to more than one living entity at a time.

Being overly preoccupied with first black man this and first black woman that is less useful in this context of multiple firsts. What we endeavor to do with this discussion is to at least help guide readers out of the box who no longer want to be limited and confined by linear beginnings. As we travel back in time to establish a connection with our origins, we have to keep in mind that time is not linear. There is no such thing as a time line. We learned this misleading description in school from linear thinking people who were taught a Eurocentric view of the world. We will cover more about time later. For now, just keep in mind that while our cosmic origin may be singular, our Earth origins may be plural. As we travel back to our beginnings, we may not necessarily travel back to one origin such as Africa. Boxed in linear thinking has even caused us to toss around the idea of Pangaea, which has been subsequently labeled Africa. This idea suggests that all of the world's land was on one side of the planet's surface. Over time, it broke up into the continents and islands we see now. What's that? Did we detect someone envisioning a world extremely out of balance? What kind of wobble do we suspect there would be if all of the rock was on one side of the surface of the planet? We do not find this to be consistent with how land is formed in the first place; but we will not pursue this line of thinking since this is totally unrelated to human origins anyway. If this ever occurred, it was millions of years before humans ever existed. So, Pangaea cannot be used to describe the primacy of Africa, or to explain humans on different continents before there were boats.

The Pangaea argument is often supported by seemingly obvious visual evidence. We are asked to look at the model of the globe and see how neatly the pieces could fit together. All the while, the thought of balance never seems to enter our minds. Let's look at a current case of land creation to see if we can arrive at more lucid details. We will start off by correcting the misnomer of creation. As far as we can determine, living things are not created, we are born. We can create pottery and automobiles, but living things are born of a Mother. This includes bacteria which reproduce through binary fission. It is still born from the womb of Mother Earth. What about terrestrial creatures? What about the land itself? Where does it come from? Consider the current case of Hawaii. Where did it come from? Is it not alive? Of course it is. It must have come from the womb of the Mother. Did it come from Africa? Did it break off from Pangaea? It most certainly did neither. Hawaii came from the womb of the Mother like all other living things on the planet. It appears that her womb is the volcano. We mentioned that she has more than one womb which is how she can give birth to more than one kind, even simultaneously. Fraternal twins can be born from different wombs like Hawaii and other islands that are still being born. Hawaii has over 100 species that are indigenous to Hawaii. Birds bring some things and humans do as well; but many life forms originated in Hawaii.

The blockage with thinking about life in this way is that we did not understand the seed, which kept us from recognizing the womb of the Mother. The movie "Roots" was fiction and the fixation on roots actually impairs our ability to understand origins. We say the Earth is our Mother as it rolls comfortably off of the tongue. The recurring trouble is that we never gave this any thoughtful inquiry. We never considered *HOW* the Earth is our Mother. Living things can evolve, but the Mother also has seeds of new living things just like the seeds of the original bacteria. This line of thinking is a paradigm shift. Notice that volcanic ash cools and hardens into bedrock. Bedrock weathers down into soil. Soil provides for the seeds of plants. Plants provide nourishment for animals such as humans. If we truly want to know ourselves and the Mother, then we need to ask her before we get too reliant on our assimilated faith in Eurocentric science. We cannot use science to explain Nature. We must use Nature to explain science. In other words, Nature must always come first if we want to be able to validate our ideas in a concrete, holistic context. As we discuss multiple origins of living things, we are expanding the emphasis to include multiple origins of human beings and multiple origins of civilization. For a more complete picture of who we are, we have to broaden our view of being children of Africa. We are children of Mother Earth, but not necessarily children of Africa. America is also a mother. Actually, America and Africa are both wombs of the same Mother Earth.

As we broaden our view, we will realize that we are also born of water. We are not just children of corn. We are also children of the Atlantic. One of the indigenous families of the southeastern U.S. was called Creeks. They did not call themselves Creeks or Indians. The invader called them Creeks because they lived near creeks as a water source. Humans are water people, not just terrestrial animals. Most of the pyramid building people in the southeastern U.S. lived near rivers. The pyramids just outside of East St. Louis, Illinois were built at the confluence of the Missouri, Illinois and Mississippi rivers.

The temple pyramid at this site is actually larger than all of the pyramids in Egypt and Africa. When we write about being red paint people of the Atlantic Ocean, it should not be surprising. The Atlantic was not a barrier for people who understood Nature. It was more like a river. In fact, it was the river currents in the ocean that facilitated the trips between the Americas and West Africa. There are also the northern currents which facilitated trips that included modern day Canada, Western Europe and Greenland. We acknowledge that this path exists, but it is someone else's story. So, we will let someone else tell it. Our story has to do with the historical and future presence of black people in the Americas.

Chapter 11

Origin of blacks in the Americas

IN order to lead up to further explanation of who blacks in the U.S. are, we found it necessary to share a brief alternative of the origin of living things on Earth. This gives us a foundation from which we can build a more useful understanding of who we are than what we have been previously limited to. We are only presenting a summary or outline of an alternative view of the world. This is the big picture. The details will be filled in by your own reading, oral history and experiences. We choose to present a world view that is liberating. There are many details that can be selected from history. We present the historical facts that lead to the freedom to become more fully human. It is our aim and our hope that after reading this book, you will be less vulnerable to European indoctrination. We are not attempting to program the masses. We put forth our best effort to liberate the masses from self-destructive programming in order to heal the people of viral infection. We can be sure that we are being made into viruses because our behavior has changed. We are aiding and abetting the destruction of the world. We have become complicit with this destruction which is suicidal because we destroy ourselves in the process. Healthy cells are not suicidal. Wind mills and solar energy are not going to stop the inevitable Armageddon. We have to change our entire view of the world from the beginning.

We will not try to recreate a beginning in Africa and come forward. Our approach is to start where we are and go backwards to look for additional insights about our origins. We find that Black Americans are ancient people. Our beginning in the space of the current political domain of the U.S. does not start with Africans in 1619 or even in 1526. Neither do we start with the

Moors or Egyptians of *They Came Before Columbus* by Ivan Van Seritma. This is a Pan-African perspective that builds on a Eurocentric view of the world. It neglects to consider where we are and what is going on in interpreting the identity of the Negroes of ancient America. In this respect, the Pan-African historical view echoes invading European sentiment suggesting that ancient Black Americans cannot be Black Americans. We have to be someone else and come from somewhere else. The artifacts and data show that so-called Negroes lived here as natives in pre-Columbian America, not as foreigners from Africa.

From St. Louis, Missouri to Miami, Florida is where most of us come from at any point in history. Our affinity for pyramids is also quite fulfilled in this Southeastern area. In fact, the oldest 11 pyramid plaza in the world is in Louisiana on the Ouachita River. These are older than Egypt and Peru. Also, in the southeast, we still use the name of the Black Warrior River that runs through Alabama. There are also pyramids on this river near Tuscaloosa which means black warrior. We also find the Calusa people in Florida. Calusa means black man. We find the musical language of the Chickasaws in Mississippi. Yes, the rhythmic, musical language of hip hop has seeds right here in this land. Blues music also has an indigenous beginning. It came from a Cherokee curing chant that was often sang when a loved one was killed or badly wounded in Tennessee and North Carolina. The only reason we are not aware that many elements of our culture stem from beneath our feet is because we have never looked. We accept the oppressor's guidance and look elsewhere for our identity.

Blacks in the U.S. also have cultural influences from south of the border thousands of years before 1619. If we consider the culture of the Atlantic, let's move in "U" shaped fashion from the southeastern U.S. into Mexico and the Caribbean. Here we find the Olmec who are the very Negroid looking ball players and the originators of the most accurate calendar in the world. It is now called the Mayan calendar. Nearly all of the achievements during this period are attributed to the Maya. In this way, the invaders can pretend the Olmec are insignificant anomalies. Afrocentrism does not help this situation. If they were African as Van Sertima assumes, then they were still anomalies. The Olmecs were not African. They were Black Americans. They were not only culture developers, pyramid builders and calendar creators. They were also children of the corn. They were indigenous to the Americas. It was originally thought that the Olmec were the Mother culture of the Americas. We now know that this is not the case. Continuing with the culture of the Atlantic, we travel southeast across Mesoamerica into the northern part of South America.

On this journey, we pick up more of the Negroid images in *African Presence in Early America* also by Van Sertima. Here we find the world's oldest high civilization in Caral, Peru. According to the physical evidence, many of the black people currently in South America are indigenous to South America. We find ancient Black Americans among the older ruins of Peru. There are pictures of some of them in Van Sertima's books. We still have the same problem with mis-identifying who these people are. The problem is so pervasive that blacks south of the U.S. border are called Latino. Just because a person speaks a Latin based language, does not make him Latin. The mis-informers try to correct this blunder by identifying them as Afro-Latinos. This does not solve the problem of an identity crisis. American culture begins with blacks south of the U.S. border. It pre-dates Latin culture and pre-dates African culture as well. To describe Americas old world as Latin America is an attempt to make a European (Latin) claim to everything south of the U.S. border except Haiti and a few English speaking spots. To call the indigenous people Latinos is to further lay claim to the persons who originated culture in these lands and waters. Latinos are Europeans. To call any other American people by this name is essentially the same as calling them slaves or mulattos. If you are black from south of the border, that does not automatically mean that you are African or Latin. What about the indigenous people? Are they invisible or just a homogenous red in color?

The second largest population of blacks in a country is not even on the continent of Africa. It is the South American country of Brazil. We are taught that all of these people were brought on European boats from Africa. Physical evidence is not actually supplied. We suspect that there is more to the story. Europeans did not have the wherewithal to bring this many people. Admittedly, there were many more Africans imported south of the U.S. than there were into the U.S. but the capabilities of Europeans who had just learned to sail the oceans has been wildly exaggerated. The ancient artifacts throughout the Americas do not show a homogenous red people as the only natives. We suspect that many Brazilians assumed to be of African descent are also of indigenous heritage. This position satisfies both sides of the equation, so to speak. It fits the scant physical evidence of European transport as well as the stone faces found in the area. It is the same game played on U.S. blacks. The invader wants to ensure that black people do not have any legitimate claims through indigenous ties to the land. This is why he destroys our identity. Connecting us to an African identity is desirable to the invader in America because our indigenous identity threatens his domination.

Moving on with the culture of the Atlantic to the northeastern bend of our "U" shape, we finally travel east across the Atlantic to the West Coast of Africa. This "U" shape marks the ancestral seeds of Black Americans. This also identifies the path of the red paint people of the southern Atlantic Ocean. Part of breaking out of the slave mentality, as taught by Dr. White, is being able to see ourselves as one people of the Atlantic as opposed to two people of different land masses. There is voluminous information available on African origins for Black Americans. This book aims to give us the West side picture of our identity and origins. Our main focus is on indigenous American identity as it pertains to Black Americans. It only differs from Pan-Africanism by starting out where we are. Further insight into the people of the Atlantic is intended to help us unify. Since most of us will remain in America, however, our discussion discounts much of our African heritage as less relevant. Recall that we must not only focus on who we are, but we must also concurrently deal with where we are and what is going on. If we intend to remain in the Americas, it is imperative that we learn about Indigenous America.

Where we are relates to our cultural and social self. When the first Africans came here before Columbus, their survival in America depended on them learning as much about indigenous culture as they could. Without this American oriented mindset, they would have starved to death like the first English attempt at colonization in Roanoke, Virginia. An African coming here from afar would only have so much food left to eat. In order to survive, he would have to learn indigenous foods and culinary habits. Very little would be recognizable except perhaps peanuts, rice and sweet potatoes/yams since these foods were common to both sides of the Atlantic. Remembering African heritage would not help the newcomers much unless they intended to invade and impose their culture on the natives as the Europeans did. There was no beef, chicken or pork in the Americas. The flora and fauna are quite different from Africa. The pre-Columbian Africans in the Americas necessarily became children of the corn. They understood where they were and apparently did not have imperial or colonizing intentions.

The same holds true for the Africans who were brought by Europeans. They understood the concept of humans reduced to resources. Those who wanted to live as human beings rather than beasts of burden left the invading Europeans to learn Indigenous American culture. Their survival instincts did not lead them back to Africa. They forged out a living on the American landscape with knowledge from the natives. Black people stem back to the original cultures in America and black people have come recently. Whether Indigenous, African or both, it is important to develop the mind-set necessary for the ecological environment where we are. In other words, the general solution of developing an Indigenous mind-set is not dependent on agreement with respect to origins. It is only necessary that we respect where we are.

As Europeans hunted Indigenous blacks and Africans, the natives often claimed them as family or as their own slaves so that Europeans could not take them away to the chattel slavery they had in mind. We will explain this later in greater detail. We are just showing here that one of the survival solutions for the original African travelers and for the Africans brought forcefully was Native American culture. Much less than 1% of displaced Africans have been able to return to a family clan in Africa. The invader shows us this kind of solution in movies like Amistad precisely because it is something that is unattainable for the masses. As mentioned, any 'back to Africa' strategy keeps us away from threatening European domination. It, therefore, keeps us from achieving liberation. We see again how mainstream programming provides us with those things that appease our desire for revolutionary struggle but impede our progress toward freedom. Recently, we have been trying to force African characteristics onto American soil in expressing our identity. This makes us invaders is a similar way as Europeans. This book tries to help liberate us from an invasive view of the world.

In this writing, we are trying to liberate our minds from a Eurocentric and Afrocentric view of the world. When we look up to the stars, we do not get an African picture. When we look down to the ground, we do not get an African picture. Why do we think Europeans call themselves American? They are harnessing the energy between the American Earth and the cosmos while encouraging us to focus on something that stays out of their way. If we want to survive in North America, then we will have to focus on indigenous identity, culture and ecology just as previous Africans have done. Then we can have peripheral discussions about African roots as it relates to unifying and trading with Africa. The unifying geography that we described around the Atlantic gives us multi-dimensional use for the "U" of unity. We see this shape in the southern path of our Atlantic heritage. We find similar language and similar step pyramids throughout this area. It is necessary for us to understand our unity as emanating from the core of our being. Envision concentric circles expanding energy outward. Black American unity begins with each other. It most closely expands to the Caribbean, then to South America and West Africa. This gives us some order to understanding unity as it is relevant to our identity.

We cannot continue to let our path across the Atlantic be narrated by the invader. He speaks of the slave trade from East to West. We choose a liberating West to East path. On this path, we do not end up in Greece or Egypt because we know that Atlantic culture is just as old, just as sophisticated and just as important. Our children have essentially been taught they are primarily from West African slaves. It is made synonymous with Black American. The Europeans who created this narrative follow the enslaving heritage to Greece. Since they typically provide the material we study, our scholars often end up in Greece as well. Since the 1960s, it has been well exposed that Grecian scholars stole their knowledge from ancient Egypt or Kemet as it is called. Although some Afrocentric scholars focus on West Africa, the umbilical cord of academic acceptance is a making a connection with Egypt because this is the origin of European knowledge. It is not the origin of our knowledge. Oftentimes, as with Rastafarians, our scholars follow the Nile River up to Ethiopia. This is the linear academic path that makes us Nubian all the way from Black American. This is also exactly where the invader of America wants us to be because we become no threat whatsoever to his continued control and global domination.

The European has been followed to Greece as black scholars use the same linear approach to find our identity in Egypt and Ethiopia. These are the bread crumbs that are left for us to find. Admittedly, Egypt retains a strong spiritual allure just as the Mayan culture in Mexico does. The enlightening symbolism, however, often does not offer enough insight to liberate us because our view of the world has been shaped by Eurocentric framework and development. We have found in the process of discovering truth that the same symbols will yield more insight when they are not confined to a linear view of the world. If we study the Western self, including the American self, before taking in an Eastern (Egyptian, Grecian) view of the world, we will have a localized identity from which to interpret Eastern symbolism.

The Egyptian path misidentifies who we are because it initially ignores where we are and starts out somewhere else. It builds on Egypt as a cultural core which expands to West Africa and then to America. If we start where we are and go backward, we will experience a different historical reality. Afrocentrism, which is built upon an Eastern foundation, becomes much less useful for black Westerners in the U.S. There is an apparent attempt to raise our self esteem by linking us to sophisticated ancestry outside of the Americas. It is reminiscent of similar reasoning used by Dr. Johanson. Just as there is no real connection between Lucy and Black Americans, West Africa is not a missing link between ancient Kemet and Black Americans. We seem to be locked into certain research parameters because we cannot get support for liberated thinking.

Consider a culture that is not overcome with assimilation or emulation. The Australian aborigines still live in their ancient culture. They couldn't care less about being called primitive or inferior. They couldn't care less about pyramids or melanin. They have no preoccupation at all with ancient Egypt. These people know who they are, where they are and what is going on. They are also fully aware that the invader is stupid, devilish and self-destructive. So they chose not to follow Europeans intellectually to Greece and Egypt. They chose to emanate from their own core. Although, they are worse off than they were before the invader came, they stand a better chance to survive because they do not have an identity crisis.

Ironically, since Eurocentric technology is destroying the planet, they are now going to the Aborigines to learn how to work with some drought resistant plants. We learn from the Aborigines that it is wise to move backward and forward from who we are where we are rather than starting from a disconnected beginning and trying to recreate who we are. We have plenty to be proud of in the Western Hemisphere from St. Louis in the U.S. to Ghana in West Africa. We do not need to go outside of the Western Hemisphere to find ourselves or our origin. We do not need to go anywhere to find cultural sophistication or to raise our self-esteem. We just need to stop judging ourselves by European standards. Understanding ourselves and our environment improves our health, behavior and survivability while Eurocentric knowledge divides and destroys us. Recall the healing process of expelling the foreign material.

One approach to staying grounded in who we are is to start where we are. In dealing with where we are, we would like to use two scholars as an example. One of those scholars is Dr. Asa Hilliard. Allow us to preface our comments by saying that he was an excellent resource in his field of educational psychology. He seemed to have fallen into the Egyptian scholar trap in the latter part of his life, however. We were present when Dr. White invited Dr. Hilliard to travel with us to some of the pyramids in Georgia. He declined. He was well aware of Dr. White's research into the identity of ancient Black Americans. For whatever reasons, he chose not to get involved. Although he declined to travel to pyramids less than 50 miles from his Georgia State University office, he made many trips thousands of miles away to the pyramids in Egypt. What leads us to look for ourselves in the East when we have clear, visible ancestors in the West with the same scale of accomplishments? Sure, there were pyramid builders in Egypt who looked like us; but there were also pyramid builders right here who looked like us. We learn thoroughly in our scholarship, but only in the direction which has already been prescribed by the dominant culture. University schooling is set up to perpetuate this structure. In contrast to the mainstream path or the slave path that leads to the Mediterranean, the southern path leads to the culture of the Atlantic. The southern path also reveals that there have been free black people in the Americas since the beginning of humanity.

We find fatal flaws with the Afrocentric interpretation of black artifacts found in the Americas as being African in origin. It is clear that the people in question were an integral part of indigenous American culture. The ethnicity of Negroid images found all over the Americas is of Black American heritage. The problem is that we have erroneously come to believe that all black people come from Africa. Subsequently, we automatically label black people found anywhere in the world as African. This reflects the fact that European schooling has successfully locked all black people into an African box. It does not reflect the real world, but it does describe the seemingly inescapable African paradigm that has been created in our minds. We notice again that it is misleading to start out from a Eurocentric one-origin premise. Just because all Europeans come from one place does not mean all black people come from one place. We are led to Africa and Egypt so that the invader can rule the world from the extremely fertile Americas.

Allow us to give one example of how Afrocentrism is made up of the crumbs that are left for us to find. Ivan Van Sertima received much of his ancient American information from the works of Alexander Von Wuthenau who wrote, *Unexpected Faces in Ancient America*. His book is built on the premise that there were Africans and Semites in pre-Columbian Mexico and Central America. It is an excellent resource of pictures for those who require visual aids to solidify an understanding of this discussion. One of our favorites is a poster entitled, "Humanitas Americana." All of the faces in this poster came from one historic site. It reveals people who look like Asians, Africans, Semites and typical indigenous Mexicans. Van Sertima's work is built on the black faces left over from Von Wuthenau's work. We respect the value of Van Sertima's work as an excellent synthesis of material from his day. We are only pointing out that there is no real departure from misinforming Eurocentric scholarship. The main idea to take away from this is that the linear, one origin history that we have been taught is confining and misleading.

Chapter 12

Mother Earth, America and Africa

IN this book, we follow the logic of a dynamic multi-origin world. We hope that as readers continue research, a more lucid perception of ancient Americans may emerge. If we allow invading Europeans to narrate what we see, then we are obviously not going to get a clear picture of an African or American identity. This is often what happens to Black American historical scholarship and partially explains why our identity has remained in the box. Boxed in thinking has effectively limited our attempts at liberation. As we delve into the history of pre-Columbian America, we are going to find at least four distinct groups of people, including so-called white people. This book is not intended to be an exhaustive history of the Americas. For the sake of brevity, we are confining our discussion to that part of the history which is liberating for Black Americans.

As we consider a non-Eurocentric interpretation of historical evidence, let us keep a quote in mind from Vine Deloria's *Red Earth, White Lies*. "The major difference between American Indian views of the physical world and Western Science lies in the premise accepted by Indians and rejected by scientists: the world in which we live is alive."[13] We are saying unequivocally that an indigenous view of the world is liberating and is more consistent with the reality that we live in. Oppositely, the illusion of history that we have been taught is an edifice of subjugation designed by invaders who attempt to dominate the globe by dominating our thinking. Allow us to reiterate that this discussion comes about because an Afrocentric view of the world has not been liberating for Black Americans. Afrocentrism builds upon too many intellectual pillars reconstructed by the oppressor. It changes some views, but not the ways of thinking that are detrimental to our sustainable survival.

Much of the information we research is going to come from European authors with a Eurocentric view of the world. As we learn to think outside of the box, we can begin to process this information from a different perspective. For example, we mentioned that finding black people in ancient America should not cause us to immediately assume that they are African. Just because Europeans provide the information does not mean we have to view it in the same way that they do. Accepting their anti-Nature, anti-life views is actually an impediment to us arriving at a truthful identity. Remember the way they see information is going to almost always support their superiority and conversely encourage our inferiority. The tricks will not necessarily be obvious. We can stay on a liberating track, however, if we keep in mind why we are being misled, how we are being misled and the importance of learning to think outside of the box. The more we learn about Mother Nature, the more we will realize that Africa is not the Mother. Africa is not the Motherland. The Earth is the Mother. Africa is only one of her wombs. Africa is only the womb of Africans. It is not the mother of all people, nor is it the mother of all black people. With a more discriminating perception of Nature, we realize that Africa is not a Mother at all. The poison of mental slavery pierces much deeper than we expected. It keeps us from connecting with each other and our Mother.

We do not understand Mother Earth or Africa because we have been intentionally misguided. Afrocentric teachings are often carefully guided and confined by Eurocentric framework. It is European invaders who disingenuously crafted the "Africa first" view of the world. We follow suit. Europeans claim one human origin for everyone with no plausible explanation at all of where they themselves come from. They certainly did not come from ancient South Africans or Ethiopians, whom their science tries to prop up as almost Homo sapiens. We have already explained that they do not come from black albinos. Europeans have no idea where they come from, so in order to appear superior they had to destroy our knowledge of origins. Then they place themselves on an academic pedestal so that they can tell us where we come from. For example, we watched a documentary on television that filmed an arrogant European going around the world with his DNA studies to further prove the theory of linear human origins from Africa. This scholar made his way to Australia. He commenced telling the aboriginal foragers about his findings. The aborigines seemed to know he was clueless upon arrival, but they patiently listened to his analysis anyway. The scientist went on to tell them that based on his DNA evidence, Australians had to come from Africa through India and unexplainably made their way to the island continent of Australia. All of this supposedly happened before there was any physical evidence of boats. We should also notice from the logic of the first section that the invaders are called Australians and the indigenous people are called something else, namely Aborigines.

The first question the indigenous Australians asked the scholar was how old his science was. The scientist's reply was around 50 years. Of course, the natives got a good laugh out of that. They no longer had to assume he was ignorant. Now, they were sure. There was an Australian in the group with some formal education. He explained that it was not possible for Australians to have migrated from India, since all physical evidence shows that Australians are older than Indians. The aborigines explained to the scholar that they were not confused about where they came from because they had an unbroken link back to their beginnings. They told him that they had been singing the same songs of their emergence from the dream world since the dawn of Homo sapiens. Beyond the shadow of a doubt, they were sure they had originated in Australia. They made it clear to the scientist that they could not have come from Africa. The Natives even suggested that Africans may have come from them. This information should help us to realize that Africa does not have the patent on blackness. We know the original people of Australia are black people. Just because they are black does not mean they came from Africa. Black people come from all around the belly of the Earth. The idea that Africa is the Mother confuses the reality that the Earth is the Mother. It further keeps us from understanding her dynamic propagation as opposed to misinformed linear migration.

The documentary we are drawing from illustrates the fact that prior to European invasion, indigenous people from all over the world were unambiguously clear about their origins. The only people in the world who did not know where they came from were Europeans. This is largely because of their disdain for their elders and Nature, while being fixated on finding the fountain of youth. They have always had and still have a Peter Pan syndrome. They refuse to grow up and follow Nature, like mature human beings. They refuse to accept that the world does not revolve around them. The only unenlightened people who thought the Sun revolved around the Earth were Europeans. The only people who act like spoiled brats who must always have their way to the point of unilateral aggression are of the European Diaspora. Using the term Diaspora makes sense for Europeans because they likely come from one place. They don't know where that place is, which explains why they would be looking in Africa. Using the term Diaspora for black people does not make sense because all black people do not come from the same place.

In another documentary entitled, "Elder Brother's Warning" produced by Alan Ereira, the Kogi observed this childlike behavior. They call Europeans "younger brother." The Kogi are unassimilated people indigenous to the mountains of Colombia. They are well aware of how Nature functions and they know European invaders of Colombia have not yet matured to the level of respecting Nature. The Pan-European Diaspora remains inferior about their origins and knowledge of the world in general. For this reason, they are extremely aggressive in destroying or changing other people's origins and knowledge. They can only be exalted to superior status if they hold more knowledge than others. To solve this problem, they destroy our past so they can create an inferior past for us. Being aware of the nature of the invader, the Kogi never taught Europeans their language. This way the invader could never narrate Kogi history or experience.

In addition to Australians, the Kogi are also historically clear about their origins. Not only do they claim to have originated in Colombia, they also claim that Colombia, as opposed to Africa, is the heart of the world. Their view is similar to the Garden of Eden in the Torah and Bible. Although we will not reduce the story to linear migrations from Colombia, there is quite a bit of evidence to support their view. The main ingredient the Kogi have to support their claim is real estate, or at least a real landscape. In contrast, the Garden of Eden story is fiction. It is Hebrew mythology. Just because this story has been forced on Europeans and all of the people they invaded does not make it true. On the other side of the world, the evidence that supports Colombia as the heart of the world still exists today. The mountains and beach and forest and desert of this area are a microcosm of the entire planet. Some of this area is rainforest, but some of it is desert, while still other parts boast more balanced amounts of rainfall and temperature. Although this is near the equator, some areas are even suitable for the polar bear. It is said that every animal in the world can find a home somewhere in this area. As Alan Ereira mentions in the documentary, this area is a copy of the whole planet in miniature.

We do not study any of this kind of material because the slaver has our minds confined to Africa and the Middle East. Black Americans, who are in the Middle East looking for their spiritual and physical origins, remain vulnerable to the limits of East African culture being applicable in America. We are programmed to look for our origins in East Africa; but we are also free to create our own historical direction. Mental freedom is the medicine that can cure our minds of viral infection. Medicine is undesirable which is on reason why very few people are likely to read this book. We have to come to terms with whether we really want to be healthy individuals and a healthy people. If we truly want to survive, then we are going to have to get our heads out of the desert sand and begin to establish our reality from the ground beneath our feet. As we start in the U.S. and take the Southern path of the Atlantic people around to West Africa, we will notice what is going on in South America, called the 'heart of the world'. If we take the mainstream mental path, which ends up in Egypt, Ethiopia or Iraq, we will not find anything liberating for Black Americans. Specifically, what we are announcing is that our identity and survival depend on us liberating ourselves from the Eurocentric and Hebrew teachings of East African and Middle Eastern beginnings, respectively. We have to tell our own story.

It could be that the Hebrews began in the Iran/Iraq/ Syria area. This is not relevant to the experience of Black Americans because we are not Hebrew, neither do we come from Hebrews. We are not related to any of the tribes of Israel, lost or found. It could also be that Egyptians began in Ethiopia or come from Nubians. Again, this is not relevant to the experience of Black Americans because we do not come from Northeast Africans. Europeans lead us to this area and entrap our minds so that they can rob the world blind from Washington D.C. Learn the game. We are being played like a chess game with none of our pieces on the board. Watch my eastern hand while I rob you with my western hand. That is the game. We are not Hebrews and we are not Nubians. We are people of the Atlantic. Because we are being taken so far away from ourselves, we have not even noticed that West African language, drumming and culture is closer to indigenous American culture than it is to East African culture. The step pyramids in West Africa are like those around the Atlantic. Before we move on to show how Colombia fits into the larger scheme of Atlantic culture, we would like to expose one of the misleading tricks used to close our minds to oral history and traditions versus Eurocentric writing and science.

Chapter 13

Oral Traditions

WHEN we were in kindergarten, we were taught to sit in a circle for an experiment in oral accuracy. A short story was told to the first person in the circle. Each child passed the story along until it reached the last child in the circle. Typically, the story had been altered by the time it came back to the teacher. This is part of the white superiority conditioning designed to discount oral traditions as primitive and inaccurate. As a result of the experiment, we grow up with a Eurocentric belief in written and scientific accuracy. We equate these methods with fact finding and thus with truth. What this experiment does not account for is adult stories that are passed on in cultures that are built upon oral traditions. Deceptively, the experiment uses children from a culture developed on phonics. For example, the Kogi in the mountains of Colombia do not use writing in the way that we do. They have been telling the stories of European invasion for nearly 500 years. Their stories are completely accurate and fully backed up by the Spanish chronicles. This demonstrates that oral traditions like those of the Kogi or those in Australia can be just as accurate as written history. The oral traditions are likely to be more accurate because the invader who writes history has every incentive to lie in order to justify his invasion. This is just as true with the Hebrews who invaded the Canaan land as it is with the Europeans who invaded the Americas.

Oral and written traditions from Indigenous Americans are not well publicized because they do not confirm the superiority of the invaders. These traditions also do not allow for Manifest Destiny or any other European invasion of the Americas to be justified. If our slavery depends on covering up this information, then our liberation depends on uncovering this information. This is one of the aims of this book. Now that we have shed a little more light on how we are being influenced, programmed and fooled, let's turn out attention back to South America. Further support for Colombia as the heart of the world includes the most recent evidence of the lost culture of Atlantis. Some people consider this primitive mythology. What we are referring to is not a fabled city at the bottom of the Atlantic Ocean. We are bringing your attention to the physical evidence just south of Columbia in the political entities of Brazil and Bolivia. There are probably more than a thousand books and documentaries about the Nile River in Africa. In contrast, there is a relatively small amount of accessible information about the Amazon in South America.

The mouth of the Amazon is in the Atlantic which makes it more relevant to the experience of people from West Africa and the Americas than the Nile River in East Africa. The people of the Amazon were just as advanced and just as ancient as the people of the Nile. There were causeways cut through the jungle to connect the tributaries of the Amazon. These were aquatic engineers who traveled everywhere by boat. They were water people who stretched from the Atlantic to the Pacific Oceans. The people of ancient Bolivia were such extremely sophisticated water people that they even used irrigation canals to grow crops in the mountains that were normally too cold to support human food plants. This gives us clues not only of the ingenuity of the people, but also of the population density. If there were only a few people to feed, they could have been fed from the crops of the warmer climates. The most recent scientific data, maps and oral traditions place the lost nation of Atlantis in the Brazil/ Bolivia area. These were not two separate political entities prior to European invasion. This was one of the most sophisticated nations the world has ever known whether we call it Atlantis or not. Of course, this was accomplished without destroying the rain forest.

Rain forest technology was not the only advancement of South America. Just West of Brazil and Bolivia, still in the area of Colombia, we find the world's oldest high civilization of pyramid builders. These pyramids were recently found under the desert in Peru. The oldest, largest and longest running civilization was found in Caral, Peru. The advancement of this culture is older than that of ancient Egypt, known as Kemet. This means that the thesis of Cheikh Anta Diop of an African origin of civilization is no longer valid. Contrary to the popular belief of Black Americans and Africans, Africa is not the origin of civilization. We are not necessarily suggesting that civilization has only one origin. We are pointing out; however, that Native American civilization is older than African civilization. The most recent physical evidence supports this fact. In light of the most recent evidence, Johanson, Leakey and Diop had great Eurocentric scholarship, but incorrect conclusions. Their story suggests that humans began in East Africa and migrated all the way around the world. The last stop in the migration theory, after crossing the Bering Strait, is supposedly South America. Somehow the last people to populate the planet created the first high civilization complete with extensive trade networks, cotton clothing and pyramid ceremonial centers. Obviously, the truth does not fit the mainstream chronological framework. The African origin of humanity is not consistent with real world interactions. The African origin of civilization has been disproved by the latest physical evidence.

Dr. White used to teach us that America was the old world. He actually taught us this even before the most recent data was available. Dr. White made his transition in the year 2000. Caral, Peru was not even found until 2001. What this shows us is that if we follow Mother Nature as our inner guide and understand how we are being misled, then we do not have to be overly dependent on European style research and archaeological findings. Besides, if they withhold information pertinent to our history, we can still embrace our true identity if we have learned how to look inside. The most important thing externally is to learn the laws of Nature. Mother Nature will tell us the truth. Teachers, Ministers and Scientists may inadvertently mislead us. The more we learn about how Nature works, the better we can remain grounded in our struggle for sovereign and sustainable survival. This will make us less vulnerable to continued domination. Dr. White had a firm grasp on the inner workings of Nature. He also understood the opposites game the oppressor plays. The invader says the East is the old world. We know the reality is closer to the West being the old world. There is also a book on the subject that we found interesting. The title is, *America-the New World or the Old?* by Werner Muller. This book is not about the Liberating "U". The author is German so his interest is in the Northern path. The basic premise of America being the old world is the same, however. In addition to transatlantic information, he also includes transpacific information. It was not the Africans who were the water people traveling all over the world. It was dark skinned people, but they were from the Americas.

It is said that a picture is worth a thousand words. We have stated that the world's oldest high civilization is in Peru. If you want to know what these people looked like, take a gander at the back cover of Van Sertima's *African Presence in Early America*. While we are on the subject of South America, we should mention that the oldest accepted physical evidence of Indigenous Americans (Homo sapiens) is in South America. These people are about the same age as Homo sapiens in Africa and Australia. There are extremely old bones found in various parts of the world that do not get publicity, but it is more important to understand the logic because older bones are found every few decades. A good source for helping us to grasp indigenous American origins is *Red Earth, White Lies* by Vine Deloria. One thing that we can be sure of is that Native Americans did not come from Asia via the Bering Strait. The Bering Strait theory is a story the invader created to set up justification for his invasion. If the Americas were devoid of human life until yellow people changed into red people and came here from Asia just a few years ago, then Europeans were not really stealing land from aboriginal people. This land was up for grabs. Europeans just came to further settle the land that was primitive and scarcely populated. If Native Americans came from Asia, then this really was not their land. Since it really did not belong to the inhabitants, Europeans were not invading. They were just coming to occupy free land. From this line of thinking, they teach our children to sing, "This land is your land, this land is my land…"

This undermining approach to programming our children is clearly part of the psychological warfare. One way we can combat this kind of aggression is to begin to train counter-slavery engineers. We must defend against counter-intelligence programs by keeping real intelligence alive. We are not referring to morbid Eurocentric illusions of intelligence, like Saddam Hussein has weapons of mass destruction. Then there is intelligence that makes nuclear bombs. Nuclear physicists are really smart right? If they are so smart, why do they make nuclear bombs? More closely related intelligence makes war on poverty, war on crime and war on drugs. We already know this means keep them poor, criminalize them and give them drugs. When we write about real intelligence, we are referring to enlightened intellect like that of Mohandas Gandhi, Maurice Bishop, Bell Hooks or Malcolm X. Human intellect alone is destructive if it is not balanced with the light of the spirit. Intellect alone reduces humans to mechanical thinking like machines. We have strayed from our discussion of Native Americans and Africans. We do not want to leave the reader with the impression that we are trying to be smarter than Afrocentric scholars. We do not lay claim to the academic credentials or abilities of these well respected people. What we are saying is that intellect cannot save us, but insight can give us an edge.

Bear with me through a short discussion on the matrix of boxed in thinking that we have been confined to. We have brought up an issue that we have learned to think like machines. Should this make us wonder whether we are in a matrix? If you are unable to tap into the creative spirit of freedom because you are mentally locked into integration with the slaver, then you are in the matrix. If you are not able to define freedom and slavery with the same amount of independence that European invaders enjoy, then you are in the matrix. If you are Black American yet you are stuck in Middle Eastern religiosity, then you are in the matrix. If you can engineer a war, like Colin Powell, but cannot engineer peace, then you are in the matrix. If you can keep the secrets of European aggression, like Condoleezza Rice, but not find the secrets to overcoming oppression, then you are in the matrix. At the end of the nightmare of living black in the U.S., if you would just rather not wake up, then you are in the matrix. After speaking with thousands of Black Americans from varying income levels over the years, it appears that most of us would rather not wake up. We are often plagued with apathy, especially if we have become comfortable with our income and associated material trinkets.

We know that waking up comes with uncomfortable responsibilities. We would have to get out of bed with the enemy, the slaver, the invader, the virus. We would have to wake up from the bridled dreams of inclusion in the slaver's system. If we awake from our slumber, we would be able to see that our Mother is being raped unceasingly and the world is dying. We have been fighting to be included into a system of rape and murder. If we wake up and wash the viral infected mucous from our eyes, we may be able to see the life supporting culture right beneath our feet. Then we will have moved from comfortable lucid dreams to a fully awakened reality. For those of us who intend to stay here, which we suspect is 99% of us, let's find out how life is supported in the Americas. We cannot accomplish this from the dream state. Only a small portion of Martin Luther King Jr.'s "I Have a Dream" speech is kept alive precisely to keep us asleep in the matrix. We have to stop letting the invader's media choose our heroes and confine their teachings. There are also many unsung heroes who gave their life fighting for freedom.

For example, we never heard of Abraham who fought for freedom with the Seminole because we have been too busy focusing on Africa.

Let us wake up and face the reality of our indoctrination that takes us away from building a future for our children where we live. We have been so boxed in and closed minded with our views of Africa that we have not even noticed that the overwhelming majority of the world's foods originated in the Americas. Why would God start humans out it Africa, yet hide most of the human foods in the Americas? Again, we see that the idea of African origins is not something that we learned from Mother Nature. It does not really matter what sources you consult. Anyone who has studied indigenous American culture knows that this is where the foods come from. If we understand that humans generally populate to the limits of their food supply, we will begin to see why the most populated cities of the past were in the Americas. There were more highly populated pyramid city states in the Southeastern U.S. than there were on the entire continent of Africa. Naturally, we are insinuating that these cities are related to the identity of Black Americans. Henry Dobyns wrote of pre-Columbian population dynamics in his book entitled, *Their Numbers Become Thinned.* There is also some discussion in this book about the abundance of Native foods. Many of these foods were not readily available as part of our eco-system. Many plants were genetically engineered into nourishing human foods by agricultural scientists like George Washington Carver. Incidentally, peanuts have origins on both sides of the Atlantic.

As we continue to awaken, we will notice that the box identified in the first section is the same as the matrix we have recently discussed. It is imperative that we stop thinking like machines, especially when it comes to growing our food. Beef, chicken and pork all came with the invader. The production of these foods is incredibly inefficient. Oppositely, we are taught that contemporary agricultural economics reflects the most superior and efficient methods. In contrast, pre-Columbian agricultural science enabled us to get more of our nutrients from plants which decreased any need to kill animals leaving us with a more efficient system than we have today and obviously more healthy bodies. Our current system of feeding ourselves is not more evolved or superior or efficient. It is European destruction. Corn, beans and squash as well as amaranth and quinoa historically provided the proteins necessary for strength and vitality. Interestingly, when we go to Black American functions where there are awakened people, we usually run into a very high percentage of vegetarians. It seems that the Black American inner experience is somehow linked to vegetarianism. This is not an African experience. Africans traditionally ate a lot more meat than the children of the corn. They did not have the plant food diversity available to them that existed in the Americas. Some of them still live with cows and drink their blood. There were no domesticated food animals in the Americas. The only domesticated animal in North America was the dog, and he was not eaten. In South America it was the llama. Civilization is directly related to agriculture, not husbandry. This is why being civil is associated with the absence of bloodthirsty behavior. It is the intentional planting of seeds that spawned mankind's ability to create large, peaceful societies.

What we are saying is that the desire to practice vegetarianism is not an African cultural trait. It is a Native American cultural trait. Visit any Black American function where there are awakened people and you will see this phenomenon for yourself. Then try to match this behavior with African foods and you will come up short. We are missing out on an awful lot of the information we need for survival because we neglect to look right beneath our feet for our identity. Most black people over 35 years old know that they have Native American grandparents. We are usually reluctant to research this part of our heritage because it does not follow the predetermined path of least resistance. Unfortunately, if your family was enslaved, then your forbears were changed from Indigenous to African by the frequent name changes that define who we are. Also, if your family went through slavery, then you will not be found on the Indian rolls. There will be no written record of your Indigenous past. This does not mean, however, that we cannot make oral and cultural connections. There were no written records of our family identity before Europeans came anyway. There were only oral and cultural connections. So, there is no need to feel inadequate if all we have access to are oral and cultural connections. Remember part of making a slave is to erase his identity. The invader wants to hold us to his written standard of proving our identity because this makes it impossible for us to connect to this land. He strategically wrote us down as slaves, not as indigenous. In fact, many of us were not written down at all.

What is inside of us will bear witness to who we are. Our cultural habits that persist to this day are a testament to who we are. Food stuffs are a part of our cultural identity. Since we have been discussing Afrocentrism, allow us to share a quote. In a college history text entitled, *The American Past* (1990), there is some discussion about native foods in comparison to African and European exchanges. The following quote emerges: "Many national cuisines depend on foods of American origin, particularly the tomato and the extraordinary variety of chili peppers that have been developed from a Mexican forbear. It has been estimated that of 640 food crops grown in Africa today, all but 50 originated in the Americas."[14] We realize that U.S. history textbooks are teeming with the lies, myths and fantasies of white supremacy. This quote, however, is not so farfetched taken in the larger context of abundant native foods. It does bring to question some of the exaggerated scholarship of Afrocentric scholars. We have seen numbers as large as 200 million who perished in the middle passage. One simple question is, what did they eat? There were not 200 million people for the taking during those less populous times. These kinds of numbers would have emptied the entire west coast of Africa and some of the interior more than 500 years ago. If we would just give some thought to soul food, we would begin to find a connection. Some critical thinkers have labeled this slave food. Digging a little deeper into the issue, we find that only the meat is slave food. The rest are mostly native foods.

We bring up the subject of native foods in the first place because it will help us to recognize who we are. We shared a quote from a history textbook which revealed that 92% of Africa's foods originated in the Americas. We challenge Afrocentric scholars to disprove this. We do not care whether it is completely accurate of not. In the process of learning about native foods, we will learn a lot about ourselves. That is what we care about. As we fully awaken, we will start to nourish our bodies and our minds with foods that help create an enlightened chemical environment. From this state of mind, we will realize, as we have stated, that Alex Haley's *Roots* was fiction. His grandmother who told him the story about **THE** African in the family was a full blooded Cherokee. Dr. White used to say that chickens do not lay duck eggs. If this is true, then a Cherokee woman does not give birth to an African baby. The child must be a Cherokee or simply of Atlantic heritage. How is it that movies were made about the African and the European in Haley's bloodline? What about everyone else in the bloodline? There was no movie made about the Cherokee in his blood. What is mainstream media trying to hide? How are they programming us? This is the same game that is played with the DNA studies. They will skip over 50 people in your family tree, or leave off entire branches to find one African to connect you to. In this way, they can tell you that you come from Ghana or Angola or Sierra Leone. How does this approach deal with that one German or Irishman in the bloodline? Does that make you German or Irish in the same way the one African makes you African?

DNA is good for getting innocent people out of jail. As far as ancestral science is concerned, the DNA game is a trick. If you have American, African and European blood in your veins, who are you? Why would you choose African if you are in America? We are led to these choices by the oppressor. We are not thinking for ourselves. We assume that African traits are dominant because we have never studied the Indigenous traits. Indigenous American culture is actually more opposite European culture than African culture is which gives us a greater ability to resist mis-education. We get caught up on color and totally miss the liberating information. For example, Europeans come from meat eaters. Most Africans do too. On the contrary, Indigenous Americans come from corn eaters. Research indigenous culture and you will not only find our cultural identity, but also the mindset to fully loosen the grip of psychological slavery. Native American's come from vegetable eating people who were non-patriarchal. Our connections also included the Sun and Earth in our understanding of family. Check out the culture of the southeastern natives and you will find the information necessary for real, rather than perceived, liberation. We covered some information on how slavery veils our indigenous identity with several impermeable layers of wickedly deceitful tapestry. Along these lines, allow us to share a passage from *The Only Land They Knew* by J. Leitch Wright.

> "More dramatic was the experience of Susan, a full blooded Creek, and her six children, all of whom belonged to Judge Lane in Nashville. A body of displaced Creeks removing to Oklahoma passed by the judge's house and spotted Susan. Realizing she was an Indian, they made signs for her to accompany them. One of her children accepted the offer, and Susan herself was on the verge of joining them. But Judge Lane pleaded hard with her not to go. He told her the Indians ate raw meat and were often nearly starved. She decided to stay-and thereby remained a Negro."[15]

Oral traditions are often backed up by written sources if we dig deep enough into the history. There is an interesting parallel of oral stories that is quite relevant to our contemporary situation. There are African stories of pale people being expelled from Africa in antiquity which landed them in Europe. This is often used to further support linear migration origins out of Africa. The noteworthy parallel is that Native Americans also have stories of pale people being expelled and sent to Europe. Interestingly, the American stories exist from the cold regions of North America to the tropical regions of South America. Recent historical records make it very clear as to why Europeans would be expelled from Africa and the Americas. Their stealing, killing and destroying have always been intolerable. The oral traditions confirm that the European Diaspora has been behaving this way for thousands of years. With this information, however, we are not trying to make any claims of pinpointing where they come from. We cannot make any conclusive statements about the origin of European people, although this has been tried by Afrocentric scholars and Elijah Muhammad in *Message to the Black Man*.

Given that the expulsions stories are widespread and consistent, we can be more conclusive about unchanged behavior. Historically, integration has unsuccessfully been tried before on at least three continental masses. The resolution in Africa, North America and South America was separation. One of the more important reasons for understanding history is to keep from making the same mistakes repeatedly. For us to succumb to integration is to make the same mistakes. Black American scholars and ministers must be held accountable for their leadership and its consequences. It is imperative that we become more keenly aware of real American history, particularly since we call ourselves African American. If we don't know the history of where we are, we are already at a great disadvantage. It is time to support those who are not committed to an oppressive government or corporations. It is time for us to support independent leadership that not only represents the masses, but is an integral part of the people. Through meetings and dialogue that involve the masses, we can select leaders from the people rather than continuing to let our leaders be chosen for us by the oppressor's media.

Chapter 14

Liberating Identity

ONCE we wake up from the dream and realize that we have to fight for independence if we intend to survive, then we can start thinking in terms of liberation. Making a connection to Europe or Africa is not liberating in America. Why do you think the invading Europeans call themselves American? They do not call themselves European. They do not talk about a European Diaspora. They have changed their identity in order to steal ours. Our identity has become that of perpetual slaves. Oppositely of Willie Lynch, who taught the making of slaves, we are introducing ideas that are conducive for liberation. We cannot make a group connection to a specific African people or place, although this is attempted with Egypt. DNA studies have not shown Black Americans to have originated from Egypt. DNA studies have connected us to some individual ancestry in various African countries. This is useless for liberation. We cannot become politically liberated as individuals. The only thing that we can be sure of as a group is that we are Black Americans. We have seeds and roots in this land. We have to learn to be proud of who we are as Black American people. We are the greatest people in the world. If we would engage in some thoughtful research of primary sources of indigenous culture, we will find the wherewithal to bring our minds out of the box and save our people.

Do not be fooled by Ebony magazine's article on Native Americans owning slaves. This was documented in the April 2008 issue (or close to this date). In the article, the only way blacks could be seen as so-called Indians are as slaves of Native people. The article only referred to the black Indians as Freedmen. This is just another blatantly negative way of attaching slavery to Black Americans. This locks us into a false reality that the only way we can ever view ourselves in this country is as slaves. This is the same destructive fiction that is typical of mainstream media. It does not matter whether it is black owned or white owned. This kind of information maintains an inferiority complex among our people. Our inferiority has been internalized which is why Ebony magazine can be used to legitimize the deception among black people. This particular issue became popular in 2007 because the Cherokee were kicking the black people out of the tribe. These blacks were also labeled as slaves. If they were doing some kind of ethnic cleansing, why were they not kicking the white people out of the tribe? If you do the research, you will find that Southeastern Natives were some of the most liberated people on the planet. There was no need to own slaves. They were not capitalist people, so what did they stand to gain from owning slaves? These kinds of questions never seem to get asked. The historical facts show a completely different picture than the historical perspective we are taught.

As with the experience of Susan described by J. Leitch Wright, we find that Negro slaves and Native Americans were many of the same people, albeit with some African influence. When dark skinned people were able to live freely, they were hunted by invading Europeans. One way to keep them from becoming enslaved was for the Native families to claim that they were already slaves. In this way, the Europeans could not capture them for the chattel slavery that generated their profits. Some Native Americans owned slaves as a way to protect the hunted blacks, not as a way to oppress them. In *Fearless and Free*, George Walton mentions that the so-called slaves of the Seminole paid less into the communal pot of the Seminole than the invading Europeans paid in taxes. The blacks who lived with the Seminole also lived on their own land and in their own houses. So, who was really the slave? We are not familiar with this information because we only focus on Africa. We have missed the majority of slavery in the U.S. if we have not learned of Davey Crockett, the Goose Creek men and other slave hunters in the U.S. It was much cheaper to hunt slaves in the U.S. than it was to import them from Africa. We have seen physical evidence of black people here long before Columbus, so the idea that blacks could only be here as slaves is inconsistent with the facts and prohibits a complete search for our identity.

The truth is that blacks lived here as human beings, free of dominance. We have been here since the beginning of humanity. Slavery came along with the European invader. Slavery is a part of who the European is. It is not a part of who we are. The origin of the name is from the Slavs of Europe. Let's look at more history of slavery that came with the invasion of North America. The first census of Mobile, Alabama counted 194 slaves. To the best of our knowledge, the first census was in 1790. Of these 194 slaves, we generally assume they were all African because we are so brainwashed by the fiction movie "Roots." The reality is that only 11 of these slaves were African. Nearly 95% of these slaves were of Indigenous origin. More slaves were hunted here than were brought here. The transatlantic slave trade that we often refer to is a holocaust that occurred mostly outside of the U.S. The Europeans who invaded the U.S. did not want to run the risk of having a majority of black people in this area. As a result, they stopped importing slaves before the largest numbers of slaves were brought across the Atlantic. We also seem to ignore that there were about 350,000 Natives that went to Europe. Compare this to the 450,000 Africans brought to the U.S. If Native Americans did not significantly alter the population of Europe, why do we claim such African presence in the U.S.?

Moreover, we never say anything about Indigenous American presence in Africa. Not only did Dr. White teach that America was the old world, he also taught that the architects of the pyramids in Egypt were Native Americans. Among other things, Dr. White was a mathematician. He found that there was no zero in Egyptian numerals. If there was, then the Romans would have used it. The Arabic numerals we use today include a zero because it was borrowed from India. Thus our number system is called Hindu-Arabic. Roman numerals did not include a zero. Neither did Egyptian or Arabic numerals. The only people in the ancient world who used the zero were North Americans and Indians. Contemporary Mayan historians, like Hunbatz Men, claim that India only had the zero because it was taken there by Indigenous Americans. This is in keeping with the idea of America being the old world. History textbooks in the U.S. give credit to Mexico and India as having developed the zero independently. It is not coincidental that both cultures are vegetable eaters. Dr. White taught that the Egyptians would not be able to do the math necessary for the ancient structures without the use of a zero.

We had been learning these things from Dr. White since around 1990. Hard data began to surface in 1996. There was a documentary put together entitled, "Curse of the Cocaine Mummies." This video documents that there were Native Americans from the Atlantic culture in ancient Egypt. We note that they were important enough to be mummified. In Muller's book on

America as the old world, which we cited previously, he writes of Western culture being brought east across the Atlantic all the way to Germany on the Northern Atlantic path. We find from "Curse of the Cocaine Mummies" that the Southern influence of Native Americans not only reached West Africa, but penetrated all the way to Egypt. The only reason this information is called a curse is because it does not fit the white supremacy paradigm. The dominant culture cannot be projected in a superior light if they are the last ones to go global. Typical of their opposite approach, they like to appear as the first ones to cross the oceans. They also want European culture to appear as Western, so they intend for the real Western culture to be invisible by completely ignoring it in history. They want history to travel from East to West so that they can appear as the bringers of civilization and culture to the savages of the West.

Interestingly, a connection similar to the American-Egyptian connection exists in European culture. Mormonism is built on the premise that Yoshua (Jesus) came to North America. If a Hebrew-American connection is possible, then an American-Egyptian connection is certainly not out of the question. All of this is based on transatlantic travels. Von Wuthenau's *Unexpected Faces in Ancient America* actually shows many artifacts with Semitic features. There are countless volumes today which document the fact that transatlantic travel occurred in ancient times. In fact, Thor Heyerdahl made the trip in the 1970s in reed boats to remove any further doubt. Contrary to the lies, myths and fantasies of Eurocentric history, Columbus was not an explorer at all. He was a follower. As previously mentioned, he followed the Moors to the Bahamas. All available data make it clear that Europeans were not the first to travel the oceans. They were the last to do so. Furthermore, early Atlantic navigation was not from East to West. Oppositely, it was from West to East. Additionally, we find West to East travel from America across the Pacific.

Since we are making it clear that oceans were more like highways than they were like barriers, it is not a quantum leap for us to wrap our minds around transpacific travel. It is also well documented that Native Americans traveled across the Pacific reaching many of the islands and the mainland of Asia. Thor Heyerdahl also made trips across the Pacific in unsophisticated boats. So, we will not spend any further time proving that it is possible. We know that ancient people did this. How else do we explain the presence of human culture in Hawaii? In a documentary entitled, "The Last Queen of Hawaii", we observe that the original people of Hawaii looked conspicuously like Black Americans, albeit without the African admixture. They looked similar to Roc the wrestler. This is because Hawaii was populated by people from America. The invader knows this. When we discuss transpacific voyages, we are not referring to the more recent 1421 voyages of the Chinese. We are bringing your attention to ancient Asian contact from Indigenous American sailors. Dr. White taught that the vertical style of writing with the screen fold books actually originated in the Americas and was taken to China along with other things.

When we mention writing, we refer to symbols that have meaning, not necessarily symbols that make sounds. Dr. White also taught that no European culture has a writing system. They are confined to phonics. The word for house, for example, is not a house. The meaning has to be arrived at through phonetic interpretation. A true writing system that uses symbols which have meaning uses a different part of the brain. It requires a different view of the world. Writing is not the only thing that traveled to China. Just as we find red ochre and foods from America all around the Atlantic, we also find American foodstuffs and pottery in China and Japan respectively. We discussed South America as the origin of high civilization. Incidentally, we find Joman pottery from Peru all the way in Japan as early as 3500 B.C. It is also clear from the Humanitas Americana poster and a plethora of other physical evidence that Southern Mexico was a hub of commerce and travel for people from all over the world. We honestly do not know whether all of these people originated here in the old world of America or if they were brought later from across the Atlantic and Pacific oceans. The most reasonable interpretation is that a combination of both is most likely. It becomes clear that the oceans were not barriers for the ancient people of America.

The people of the South American Amazon and the people of the Caribbean went everywhere on water. These were not land locked Europeans who could barely cross the Mediterranean. Native Americans knew water inside and out. They did not have to arrive at ocean travel through experimentation by traveling close to the coast. They approached ocean travel through an understanding of rivers. There are rivers in the ocean. Since there are pyramids on the Mississippi River larger than all those in Africa, we do not want to minimize the knowledge of our own forebears from Missouri to Florida. The Gulf Coast was also part of the ocean traveling Atlantic community. As a testament to extensive water knowledge, Billy Bowlegs, who is from this area, was an Indigenous hurricane forecaster who needed no machines. We still do not understand water today as much as our forebears understood it then. If we did, we would not be polluting and evaporating our fresh water supplies. We would not be dumping gallons of chemicals in our water supplies just to make them suitable for drinking. This is not high tech. This is high ignorance. As a further example, allow us to mention that the Inuit of Alaska have twelve words for frozen water (ice). In English, there is only one. Although we are discussing the South, we acknowledge that the Inuit traveled across the Atlantic and Pacific Oceans as well. We have learned about the Vikings and Norsemen who came to Canada before the time of Columbus. These were still latecomers with very little knowledge of the world. Learn the Westside story and it will open up an entirely new perspective for you.

Since we brought up Pacific travels, many of us have not realized that we look a lot like people of the South Pacific. When they needed people for the movie, "Conquest of Paradise", why did they go all the way to Polynesia? The cast was for people of the Bahamas. At the time of Columbus, it was called Guanahani and the people called themselves Taino. There are Taino who still live in the area, particularly in Puerto Rico. So, why would the invader skip over all of these people and feel comfortable with going all the way to Polynesia to find some dark brown people for the cast? What are they trying to hide? In the process, what are they revealing? Do the Taino look too much like Black Americans? The invader wants us to believe that they killed all of the original people of the Caribbean. They lied, yet again. Although there were many more Africans imported into the Caribbean than into the U.S., still everyone in the Caribbean is not African. Jan Carew, the black man who wrote, *Fulcrums of Change* is also of Indigenous heritage. The invader wants us to believe all blacks in the U.S. are from Africa so that we will never fight for our rights to this land as they did in Jamaica, Haiti and the Bahamas, etc. This is how our slavery is perpetuated in this land. He keeps us focused on Africa so that we will never think of political independence here as our cousins in the Caribbean have done.

Hopefully, we are beginning to see why Afrocentrism is not liberating. Bringing these identity tricks closer to home, we have the same problem with the movie "Pocahontas" as we had with the movie "Conquest of Paradise." Why would they need to go all the way to the Philippines to find a face for a southeastern Native American? Are the Cherokee invisible? Did they not look like the Powhatans? Speaking of the Cherokee, why are the Cherokee dolls so dark but the contemporary Cherokee do not look like that? The Cherokee know that their ancestors were darker. The people today look almost like Europeans. The identity of the original people is obviously being masked. As long as the invader gets everyone to believe that the indigenous people are made up of only the ones he wrote down on paper and put on reservations, then he can always keep control of this land. By design, Indians from reservations make up a very small part of the population. Without including Black Americans and the darker Mexicans, the numbers are quite insignificant, around 1% of the U.S. populace. When we take into account the food stuffs, the pyramid city centers and the extensive trade networks, we begin to realize the population density of this area was far greater than can be explained by today's limited number of Native Americans. This reduction to 1% of the current population makes no sense in light of the purposely omitted historical data we have discussed.

We realize European illnesses took an extreme number of indigenous lives, but still a host of lies have been told to create the demographic scenario that exists today. Of course, the U.S. government is not going to recognize any people as Native Americans who can jeopardize their dominance and control. This is the same motive we have described throughout the book. The divide and conquer strategy is in full effect with the naming and classifying of non-European groups. One of the first things to question is how do we know the people on the Indian rolls are Native American? When George Catlin was commissioned to draw the pictures of Native Americans that we see in the history books, he drew pictures of Europeans. When they wanted to steal the Macon Plateau in Georgia, they bought it from Chief McIntosh. This man was not a Native American. He was a European invader. He was first cousin of Governor Troup of Georgia. In fact, the real natives killed him after they found out what happened. So that the invader could play both sides, he included many so-called white people on the Indian rolls. In this way, he couldn't lose. He infiltrated the natives so that he would have someone on the inside to bargain with. This was only made possible because Native American is not limited to a racial identity. Take some time to research the way the Natives fashioned themselves in the ancient pottery and this point will become clear.

We are aware that we have been taught to ridicule our so-called Indian blood. We know that Natives are dark brown people but we have been taught that all Indigenous people had straight black hair. This issue alone accounts for the greatest barrier to understanding our identity. We are expected to believe that there was not one kinky-headed person anywhere in the Americas until slaves were brought, or until a few Moors came. If you follow up on the research introduced in this book, it will become clear that kinky headed people originated all around the belly of the Earth, including the Americas and not limited to Africa. We are not trying to steal the glory of the so-called full blooded Indians. We are simply removing the veil so that we can see America more clearly. Artifacts from all over the Americas show evidence of straight-haired and kinky-haired natives. Dark-skinned native city dwellers of the southeast were hunted, displaced, enslaved and robbed of our lands and history. This group became mixed with African blood and called Negroes. We still have a few Native stories left in our bloodline. Indigenous people who were not enslaved were infiltrated by Europeans, marched to Oklahoma and left for dead. In the West, there were Natives who migrated from Mexico to Utah. These people were hunted like buffalo and robbed of their lands as well. This has created friction in the U.S. where the propaganda convinces us that Mexicans are foreigners.

There is ample evidence that red and black people lived here in relative harmony as one people of various shades of brown. Rather than being divisive, we would like to reconnect with Mexicans and reservation Indians who have love for Mother America. We obviously have a common enemy. The invading European virus has infected us all. To the federally recognized Indians, who only make up 1% of the population, we must add millions of Mexicans and Black Americans. These people are not foreigners or invaders. Even the Africans who were brought were part of the Atlantic community who had pre-Columbian presence here. The foreigner is the European invader. We must unite against the destruction of our Mother and our families. Otherwise, there will be no place for our children to live. In the final analysis, Afrocentric thinking amounts to little more than a mental escape. If you can escape, that's fine but it leaves the masses of our people stuck here dealing with the harsh and inhumane reality of oppression. If the black people with the intellectual and financial resources leave, it actually makes it worse for those who remain. Escapism is actually not fully possible because if we do not deal with the problem here, we are not safe anywhere in the world.

How many African countries have nuclear weapons? U.S. leaders have made it clear that if you do not have nuclear weapons, they will invade you and put down any attempt to compete with them. The only way you can be safe in Africa is to stay in your place, or at least to stay in the place of some other country's sovereignty.

It is unfortunate that we have been taught to love Africa but hate Black America. Even after being pumped up with sophisticated African self esteem, we still harbor an inferiority complex as the sold, weak and detached slaves of African descent. Afrocentrism becomes just another badge of slavery as we become subjects of another continent without any ties to a particular place on the continent. Most of our names remain badges of slavery, although we are making some progress in this area. The religions we practice are clearly badges of slavery. Our schooling is a badge of slavery. Our clothes are badges of slavery. These badges of slavery are perpetuated by our refusal to look beneath our feet and inside of ourselves for our identity. Connecting to Egyptian heritage does not solve the problem of our identity crisis. This knowledge is incomplete at best and violates all three pillars of this section. It does not represent who we are, where we are or what is going on. While Europeans did steal and learn a great deal from Egyptians, it was the invasion of the Americas that has enabled them to pursue global domination. American physical, spiritual and mental resources provide them with the cosmic and land based power to dominate. If we begin to understand who we are and figure out that we have a human right to political independence in this land, it will change the balance of power in the entire world.

Previous studies, which can be put together from the references in this book, reveal that a very large percentage of Black Americans have Native American forbears. As we go looking for our ancestral genes in the DNA labs, let's keep in mind whose science we are following. We must stop letting the oppressor define who we are. When they test for Indigenous blood, they are testing against that 1% pool of federally recognized Natives. The history of our circumstances show the only way so-called Indians were permitted to stay on their land in the southeast after being officially removed by the Federal Relocation Act of 1838 was to become Negroes. We have been labeled by several other names since then. Given that European invaders are taking over the cities again, we are likely to get another name change since we have been most recently called inner city or urban people. The only way to stop the continued abuse is to identify ourselves for ourselves. Just because some of us have African blood, this does not change us from being Black American any more than having some European blood changes us from being Black American. The more we learn about Indigenous American history, the more we will understand about Black American history and identity. There is evidence of Native Americans more than 200,000 years old. You will not find this information in African American studies. Neither will you find it in Eurocentric history. The information is not presented to you in your education because it could wake you up and bring you out of the Matrix.

Let us continue to look at how the history game is being played. Many of the stone heads that Van Sertima published pictures of are from Von Wuthenau's private collection. The multi-ethnic "Humanitas Americana" poster that we referred to has pottery and stone heads from Von Wuthenau's private collection. Many of the Negroid artifacts from the U.S. are part of private collections here and abroad. For example, when Stone Mountain Georgia was looted, the evidence was taken all the way to Germany. When tomb robbers find golden figurines and very old pottery, they often sell it to the highest bidder. They do not necessarily give it to museums in an effort to do a good deed. Museums are good resources but they are often the last places to collect useful artifacts. Our ancient Black American history is being kept out of our sight in order to perpetuate our identity crisis. Many ancient American artifacts are held in Europe as part of their National Treasure of loot. The few books from Mexico that survived the burning are being held in Europe and they are referred to by European names such as the Dresden codex. We have to expand our limited, linear view of the world in order to broaden our view of Homo sapiens, Native Americans and Black Americans. For reasons of long term survival, we have to change our view of the world into an assessment of the facts that is liberating.

It is little known that there are stone tools in Mexico over 250,000 years old. If this seems unreasonable, consider that while Europeans thought the Sun revolved around the Earth; the ancient Mexicans had already calculated the roundness of the Earth, Sun and Galaxy as we proceed around the black hole. Not only was the roundness calculated, but the imperfections like the wobble of the Earth were also accounted for. The wobble makes a 26,000 year circuit. The precession of the equinoxes takes 26,000 years to complete. Also, the center of the black hole in our galaxy is about 26,000 light years away. This understanding of the galaxy and the black hole was written in stone in ancient Mexico. The recent fuss over the 2012 calendar end date is from this part of the world. It is the end of a 26,000 year cycle. Given the far more sophisticated understanding of the world, it is likely that Native Americans got a much earlier start on civilization than Europeans. As far as the Mayan calendar end date of 2012 is concerned, it would be useful if more people investigated the star patterns confirming this date for those who are so inclined. There may be error in converting to the Julian and then Gregorian calendars. Look up Fred Martin and Native American cultural philosophy for further study of Mayan dates.

Using knowledge of our galaxy, the Olmecs played out cosmic drama from their understanding of the heavens in ritualistic ball games passed down to the Izapans, Mayans and others. These were blacks in Mexico who originated not only, the calendar and pyramid building in North America, but also developed the ball games with the help of the rubber tree in the area. These games were also played in the Southeastern U.S. where we come from. We still play similar games, yet we have no idea what they mean or even what the ball and goal represents. As a result of hundreds of years of torture and terrorism from invading Europeans, we play ball games to entertain the slaver.

We no longer have knowledge of Nature and the Cosmos woven into our culture. This partially explains how we have become so vulnerable to a continued identity crisis that allows us to join forces with the invader in destroying the world. We have come to think it is impossible to overcome our plight. It may be impossible with an identity crisis. As our identity is restored, however, our ingenuity becomes unlimited as it was when we were pyramid builders. We can become fully liberated and fully human as we come beyond the mental, emotional and spiritual limitations of the dominant cultural paradigm. As we truthfully solve the problem of our identity crisis, we can become free. Building on the idea that truth will enable us to become free, we will proceed from the core of our galactic home to a discussion of liberation theology.

Part 3

Restoring Identity

"Anytime you turn on your own concept of God, you are no longer a free [person]. No one needs to put chains on your body, because the chains are on your mind. Anytime someone says your God is ugly, and you release your God, and join their God, there is no hope for your freedom until you once more believe in your own concept of the deity. And that's how we're trapped. We have been educated into believing someone else's concept of the deity."[16]

Dr. John Henrick Clarke

CHAPTER 15

LIBERATION THEOLOGY

IN the previous sections, we wrote about solving the identity crisis in terms of who we are. We introduced some commonly omitted information about where we are. We offered an alternative perspective on what is going on in terms of the motive, the desired outcome and some of the methods used against us. One of the broad methods of oppression is to take full advantage of the psychology of human nature against the dominated group. One of the ways this is perpetuated is through locking people into a boxed in belief system...a spiritual prison of sorts. Systems of religious belief are very powerful tools of control. Used methodically, they can achieve almost machine like precision in behavior control. Once people are spiritually and mentally disconnected from their original thread of life, they become vulnerable to the trappings of the bottomless pit. According to the box that we defined in the first section, Christianity is the primary religious belief system that is used in the U.S. We do not need to do any further scholarly research to be able to see that Christianity is anti-liberating for Black Americans overall.

The fact is that we have been in bondage every since we have known about Christianity. Therefore, Christianity cannot qualify as liberation theology. Actually, no East African or Middle Eastern religion can liberate Black Americans. That is not to say that churches and mosques have not provided some solace and protection in times of great need. I do not want to discount the efforts of the Nation of Islam and some Churches whose ministries have liberated many prisoners. These efforts are commendable, although not sustainable. Charlie (the invader) can lock up many more people than we can spend the money to free as long as he remains in control of our politics and justice. In this discussion, we will try to deal with a broader view of liberation wherein we can defend ourselves from being prisoners of foreign invasion and domination. What we want to build on is the spiritual nature of the invasion and trickery so that a lasting solution to liberation can emerge. We have to regain control of the education and spirituality of our children through jurisdictional sovereignty. This is where we need to understand the bishop on the chess board that we alluded to earlier. It represents spiritual control in the game of life (which is really not a game).

We implied that the bishop became an integral part of the invasion and the subsequent slavery of indigenous and imported peoples. Christianity was not brought to save our souls. To the contrary, it was used to disconnect us from God and capture our souls as an early step toward making us slaves. Capturing souls made people easier to subdue and control. When you control a man's religion, you don't have to worry about his thinking. He is confined to your religious box. As we journey beyond belief into the realm of verifiable truths, we find that Christianity is part of the box of domination. It is part of the bondage that denies our liberation. Very large numbers of people can be controlled by belief systems whether they are imposed or indigenous. Invaders use this knowledge of human nature to effectively destroy the victim's connection to God and replace it with a subordinated connection to the invader. Our spiritual understanding has been replaced by the world view of the slaver. Our sanctuaries essentially become temples of slave indoctrination.

We have heard 99 excuses from ministers who are well aware that our connection to God was replaced by a connection to the slaver. The end result is continued bondage. They continue to teach the slaver's religion every Saturday or Sunday in spite of the obvious and well documented history that suggests this practice perpetuates the problem. Some of those excuses center around Christianity being an African religion. The problem is that this does not change any of the facts about the nature of America's invasion or the nature of a liberating response. One of the things that we have learned through this process of dialogue with our people and observing their actions is that emotions are much stronger than intellect in the human family. We follow a herding instinct rather than using the brains that God gave us. This is what leaves us vulnerable to being easily manipulated through the malicious use of belief systems. Christianity was tortured into the Black American family by the most violent means. We let our freedom-fighting forebears die in vain as we rush to remember the past figures, spiritual and political, that have been popularized by pernicious corporate mediums.

Belief is a powerful organizational and motivational tool. It is unfortunate that we have allowed our beliefs to stray so far from facts that we can validate as truth. This, of course, is working against us. We brought up many pertinent facts about how the European invasion has affected our lives. We concluded that the solution must involve full human independence. As a result of hundreds of years of repression, we have come to believe this is impossible. In this section, we will begin to explain how it is possible. We have to come to terms with the fact that many have learned to believe the oppressor is greater than God. Black Americans have not been practicing a belief in God. We have been practicing a belief in religion. With any faith in God, we would know that we can become independently free right here in this land.

We do not have any desire or faith in spiritually or politically independent outcomes partially because we have not been working with adequate spiritual framework. Our description of God is passed down to us by the same people who invaded us. It is no mystery why we may be having some trouble getting free. It has been very difficult for us to achieve any form of solidarity because we have not spiritually freed our minds. Just because previous attempts at liberation did not succeed does not mean that freedom is impossible to achieve. The torture and terror that brought us Christianity can be overcome. Rather than acquiesce in the face of spiritual fear, we can define for ourselves who God is. This can open us up to further being able to define freedom for ourselves. We currently learn that all things are possible with God except, of course, overcoming European domination. So, we realize all things are not possible with the illusions of God we have internalized. In this section, we are going to address this issue by sharing several relevant descriptions of who God is.

The struggle for freedom begins with emotional independence. Emotional self-control will enable us to move toward spiritual independence. Spiritual liberation will make possible all other areas of independence and show us how to be free to live in harmony with Nature. In order to re-connect with our own spirituality, we will have to come out of the box and out of the matrix of perpetual slavery. We have our own story of our beginning. We are not Hebrew. We are not Arabs. We are not Egyptian. We are not Moors. It is important to understand that we are not Egyptian or Moors because this still leaves us vulnerable in a subtle historical way. We were not Egyptian slave owners or Moorish invaders of southern Europe. We are not reaping bad karma for something we did to Hebrews or Europeans in the past. European aggression in West Africa and the Americas has been unprovoked. Just as on the chess board, white always moves first. What we are saying specifically is that Christianity, Islam, Judaism, Egyptian spirituality and Moorish science are all impediments to liberation for Black Americans. The first three stem from the fourth, but this is still unrelated to who we are.

We have found that much of the Bible came directly from the Egyptian Book of the Dead. This should not be surprising given that Bible scribes wrote of Moses receiving his theology training in Egypt. He did not accept Egyptian religion per se. He attempted to rely on ancestral Hebrew teachings, but these were few. With a stand on scant ancestral theology, he led his people out of servitude. It was not until after this time that he began to mix in more of the Egyptian spirituality because this was apparently all that he knew. We are not necessarily trying to emulate the struggle of Moses; but it is a commonly known story that illustrates liberation theology. Let us share how this relates to our struggle for freedom.

The part of the story that we find most useful is that Moses used ancestral spirituality to overcome physical slavery. This approach can be referred to as liberation theology. It does not really matter whether the story of Moses is exactly correct as printed in the Bible. It may even be mythology. Later, we will get into some further discussion about why it can be okay to use mythology (like complex numbers) to solve problems, as long as our positions can be supported by logic and Nature. Given the complexity of European invasion and the effectiveness of belief system bondage, we find liberation theology to be the best non-violent approach to begin overcoming oppression. It provides us with a real foundation in a bottomless pit of illusions. Since we defined liberation theology as ancestral spirituality, we will further define our ancestral spirituality as Animism. Some of you will note that this is very similar to Egyptian views. We do not disagree with that. We already mentioned one problematic subtlety. Another issue is ignoring where we are. In example, for an African in Mexico, Mayan spirituality is more practical and necessary than Egyptian spirituality. The same is true for Black Americans who have seeds in the Southeastern U.S. Local idiosyncratic practices are an important part of the whole ecological picture. Religions are ecologically specific. The spirituality and rituals of desert culture are typically not the same as those of a rain forest culture.

In another example, pastoral people do not have the same view of the world as corn people. In the desert conditions of the Middle East, animals had to be slaughtered almost daily for the survival of the people. There are not very many edible fruits, nuts and vegetables that grow in a sand desert. The people of these regions necessarily developed a kill to survive mentality. In the temperate and tropical forests of the Americas, this was not the case. The staple was corn. It was not sheep or goats or rams. The fertile Nile valley certainly provided some vegetation but the presence of wheat did not make Egyptian civilization a forest culture. It is very important to understand where we are and to respect the rules of engagement with the other life forms in our ecology. Our spiritual ignorance has allowed people to impose desert rules in our forests which have been, not surprisingly, destructive. Conversely, forest rules are inadequate in the desert. The lifestyle and religious views of southern forest people is based on plants. This less aggressive lifestyle would leave much to be desired in the desert. The relationship we have described is not as cut and dry as it may seem, however. The rules of a soil desert are also different from those of a sand desert. If you can provide water, the hard baked floor of a soil desert will still provide food.

For example, Americans like those of the southwest prayed for rain, not for the killing of animals. The religious practices included ritualistic rain dancing. The Book of the Hopi is a good source for southwestern spiritual views. They have their own creation story, religious views and ritual practices. These people were blue corn eaters, which became an improved protein source when lime salt was added in the processing. In contrast, there are also indigenous American people from wetlands and rain forests. Naturally, these groups will not have a rain dance among their ritual practices. We are just illustrating that religious practices are ecologically specific. Joseph Campbell is a good resource for information on myths and religious views from all over the world. Studying his work is one of the most efficient and nearly unbiased ways of learning comparative religion. We only need this training because our spirits have been clouded over with darkness and locked into white boxes of religious autopilot. This labyrinth of confusion makes us fit only for herding, not for independent thinking or connecting with Nature or the cosmos.

The main principle that we discussed in the last section also holds true in this section. Middle Eastern religious views do not reflect who we are, where we are or what is going on in the Americas. We do not come from there. We are not Hebrews, Arabs or Egyptians. These religious views are not part of our spiritual heritage. There is an Egyptian-Native American connection, but not an Egyptian-West African slave connection. In other words, following the West African slave path from the U.S. that has been laid out for us by the invader does not lead back to Egyptian royalty. Please understand the context for this spiritual solution. The people brought from West Africa and the people caught in the Americas were people who had few weapons and little, if any, immunity to European diseases respectively. Two characteristics are inferred, social harmony and health. In the case of West Africa, the displaced people had not created sophisticated weapons because there was no need. The lack of weaponry tells a story of the level of harmony in the social structure. Creators of harmony don't need extreme weapons. The idea that the people who were captured were weak, primitive losers is very one-sided and incomplete. The same is true for Indigenous Americans who were caught and changed to Negro and then to African Americans. Because the people succumbed to the illnesses does not mean that they were weak, defenseless losers. The biological invasion is actually a sign of how advanced in health the people were. They were not accustomed to living in the filth that the slaver brought with him. Knowledge of the major religious views in the U.S. came along with invasion. It has become an integral part of the slave culture of Black America. We proudly wear these badges of slavery as we journey to the temple every Sunday. Sand desert religious rules have allowed for the destruction of America's people and her ecological balance. This is not just a matter of our opinion. It is something that has already happened and continues to happen. The tentacles of this destructive paradigm span the globe. It is not confined to our limited discussion of America. We allow this to continue largely because it is reinforced by imposed cultural habits and a Eurocentric interpretation of a desert people's religion.

We are actually several cultures removed from these imposed political, religious views that were never spiritual in the first place. We start out with Hebrew scripture, which is outside of reality beginning with Genesis chapter 1. Then we get a story of an enlightened Hebrew named Yoshua, which is interpreted and elaborated by Paul. We call this Christianity even though it is based on the teachings of Paul. It is finally peppered by suicidal destruction as interpreted from the last book, which is Revelations. As we accept this suicidal behavior, global destruction becomes a self-fulfilling prophecy. We have learned to believe that it is supposed to happen. The world is supposed to be destroyed by mankind. We assume it is a foregone conclusion since it was prophesied to happen. Meanwhile we have no faith in the Godly principles of liberty, peace, harmony or balance. Christianity gives us something religious to hold on to, but it does not provide us with anything true or spiritual. In Red Earth, White Lies, Vine Deloria wrote "Christianity was not designed to explain anything about this planet or the meaning of human life"[7] and "Christianity has been the curse of all cultures into which is has intruded."[17]

Let us qualify this discussion by saying that we have great respect for the Shrine of the Black Madonna as a Black Christian Nationalist organization. We also have great respect for the Nation of Islam as they are also Nationalists. As an independent nation, we are likely to have several religions, but that does not change any of the facts that we have presented about truth, spirituality or ecological balance. There are some other major issues with these sand desert religions in addition to being ecologically inappropriate in the Americas. They are politically structured to be inequitable and divisive. We mentioned in the first section of the book about the inequitable problems of hierarchy that sanction a superiority complex. We were once told by some door to door Christians that God's hierarchal structure had God at the top (and maybe some favorite angels) with humans just below, leaving all other creatures to occupy the bottom ranks. This presumes we are the only sentient, intelligent or spiritual beings on the planet. Our response was if they could show us a top and bottom to the sky, then we would acknowledge this as a credible, spiritual or Godly structure. The framework that we have been confined to is illustrated as follows:

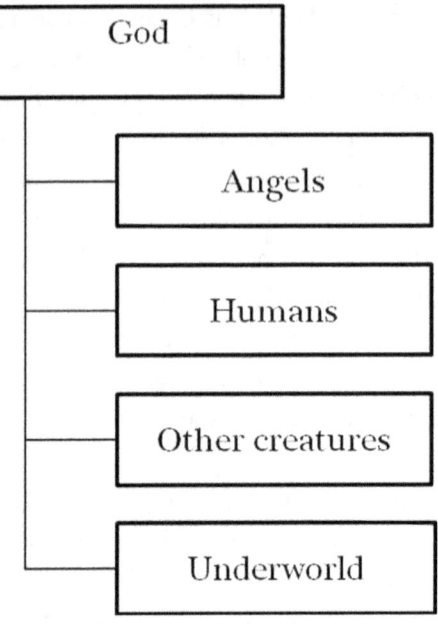

This is not God's structural hierarchy. This is a patriarchal socio-spiritual design by egotistical men who want power and control. In this paradigm, God is actually made an imaginary abstraction. Angels become a mystical fantasy. The ego ultimately rears its ugly head as Man becomes the supremely dominant player in this hierarchy. God becomes confined to what man writes in his holy scripture. In the midst of this deception, mankind gets split into two categories where the European Diaspora is superior and other humans are beneath them, but still above other animals. The Devil is apparently a resident of the underworld. This kind of social construct may be fine for the European Diaspora and chimpanzees. For Black Americans and Orangutans, it is not representative of the natural world in which we live. For this reason, it has not been a balanced, peaceful and harmonious world view. If we do not understand Nature, we will not understand ourselves. Nature is a connectedness of all living things. Mother Nature is the Mother of all living things. This is part of understanding who we are. The breadth of our being extends beyond the human family. If we understand the breadth of who we are, then we will understand why animals are also people. All of Earth's children are on the same plane of existence, or perhaps we should say sphere of existence.

We have known forever, but science also concedes that our future is inextricably connected to all other living things. We know about the butterfly effect, but it does not motivate us beyond our apathetic state of mind. If we kill a butterfly in the U.S., it may affect the weather in China… and we don't care. We have no knowledge or love of our spiritual selves, which makes it easy for us to disregard our own domination and destruction. We have been disconnected from other living things so that we could be rearranged as being below all other people. Black people all over the world are not seen as the original people. We are seen as the most primitive people and the least evolved. Nothing is going to change as we continue to do the same thing every Sunday. We are connected to all other living things, not just pale people who gave us a slave connection to Jesus. We have to understand the breadth of who we are and call upon the power of Life to enable us to live as humans in harmony with other living things. The hierarchy, domination and individualism that have replaced our cultural view and most of the subsequent technologies are driving us into extinction. This is a spiritual problem. If we get our spirits in order, we will not allow this to continue. Apathy will cease to be an option.

The breadth of our being extends to all of Earth's children. Similarly, the depth of our being extends into the past and the future. We are not made up of all those who came before us. We are all those who came before us. As previously explained, it is imperative for our survival that we understand who we are. In the Mayan language, there is a phrase spelled "in lakech." To the best of our knowledge, this phrase means, 'I am another yourself.' It doesn't make much sense in English because English speakers see the world as, 'I am superior to you.' Based on this discussion, 'in lakech' could be used to describe our relationship with our parents. We only see some of our parents in our phenotypes, but we are all of our parents. This is why we can pass on any of their genes. From a child's perspective, we are our parents. From a parental perspective, we are our children. This is the depth of our being and explains our connectedness through time. We will cover more on this when we get to the concept of everlasting life. At this point, we should at least recognize that given our spiritual ineptitude, a wise and omniscient being would not have put us in charge as the Bible suggests. We were not given dominion by God over other living things. Instead, we have a responsibility to live in harmony with other living things not as superiors, but as coinheritors of the planet. It would behoove us to emulate the ways of those who have proven to know how to cohabitate with other creatures rather than emulating the ways of those who dominate other creatures, which tends to be self-destructive. Let's take a look at another diagram. A more spiritually and historically correct view that has proven to be more harmonious is the following:

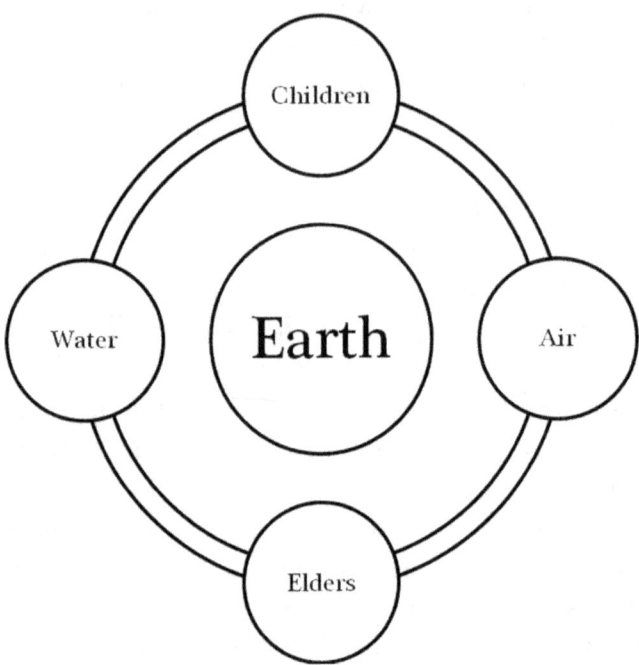

This is a universal diagram which represents the four directions, the four winds. In this diagram, people are connected to other living things in space and time without hierarchy. Water people, Earth people and Air people are connected on a horizontal plane rather than a vertical plane. Fish, terrestrials and fowl share the same plane of existence as humans, which is why we are all called 'people' in indigenous languages. The vertical plane represents a journey through time. We see the Elders at the bottom, some of whom are in the underworld which we call ancestors. Placed beyond the realm of our short time on Earth are the children who represent our future and perhaps the cosmic realm of possibility. Obviously, parents are in between the time of the elders and the children, but are not explicitly labeled in the illustration. This circular figure has no top, bottom or hierarchal implications. It represents spherical relationships like the Earth, the Sun and the Galaxy. God is not a hierarchal King or a Superior in this diagram. These are man's egotistical flaws that we have erroneously ascribed to God. In the diagram above,

God is in the center. There is nothing spiritual, natural or peaceful about a hierarchal mentality. It distorts our mental balance and retards our ability to function harmoniously with each other and with other creatures in Nature. It inflates a destructive ego and provides the foundation for the development of insatiable greed.

A hierarchal view of the world is political. The patriarchal scribes of the Bible wrote down that God gave them dominion over other animals and women because their over inflated egos had been poisoned by a superiority complex. This is not the spiritual structure of God. This is the political structure of men who want power and control. They use God to establish credibility, to dominate by using their own words. We are told it is the word of God. It becomes such a ridiculously false sense of reality that the scribes go on to write in the Bible that man comes into existence first, and then woman is made from man. Obviously, this is not how it happens in the real world. These scribes had no regard whatsoever for truth, even symbolically, in this view of the world. In establishing a liberated view, we will have to learn to discern between spirituality and politics. Just because something political is written in a religious book does not make it spiritual. We have experienced how this hierarchal view of the world is classist and divisive.

With this world view we can see how the dominant religion in the U.S. is an exclusive club of murderers and thieves. But they go to church on Sunday and ask for forgiveness. Chaplains even go with the military troops so they can pray for genocidal victories like David did in the Bible. We say the club is exclusive because you have to be Christian to join this heavenly club of invaders. Everyone else is going to hell according to the divisive opinions of the dominant group. The highway of holiness is confined to the political dogma in their chosen scripture. Hierarchy, exclusivity and patriarchy are a volatile mix of religious beliefs. It is partially the belief systems of the Middle East, including Christianity, that perpetuate the divisiveness and maintain the tension that prohibits peace. From this volatile mix of religiosity, the problem is worsened after filtering through an aggressive European interpretation as it was brought across the Atlantic. As Black American slaves and/or subjects, we ended up with extremely poor religious teachings after our own teachings were tortured out of our forebears. It is primarily this poverty of spirituality that perpetuates our financial, social and emotional poverty, hence the importance of liberation theology.

In the first section, we introduced the idea that patriarchy was a major problem. For further study on why patriarchy is so terrible, we encourage you to follow up with reading some material from bell hooks. Any woman can find reasons to be a male basher given that we have made such a mess of the world. Bell Hooks, as an author, is well researched and well balanced in her approach to patriarchy. Suffice it to know that patriarchal culture is one of the main ingredients of the destruction of the planet. It would behoove us to correct this problem, particularly in our belief systems, but also in our educational and economic systems. Patriarchy may have a proper place in some ecological regions of the Earth. It may be useful for desert cultures to be dominated by men. For the forest areas where we come from, it is inappropriate. Not understanding the Mother of a family shows a lack of understanding Mother Earth and a completely opaque view of the womb of heaven (Cosmic Mother) which are directly related to building a sustainable view of the world. Our regional and ecological settings affect to some degree how we develop our cultural traits in the first place.

In a sand desert environment, the man controls the proteins by slaughtering animals. He is associated with the source of life and God is seen as a Father. In the forest, the woman controls the proteins through the planting of seeds and/or the gathering of nuts. She is associated with the source of life and God is seen as a Mother. This is fine as long as we respect each other's culture. When we start to impose a religious view in a different ecological region, it becomes a problem. One way to get beyond this problem is to seek truths that are universal in Nature rather than being confined to views that are regionally specific. Obviously, religious rules like what to eat and what to wear are specific to the environment. For example, the foods mentioned in the Bible did not even exist in the Americas. The clothing needed to protect from sandstorms is not necessary in the forest. These kinds of rules are not universal. The idea that one group's religious rules are appropriate for all people everywhere is not consistent with peace and harmony. If truth, peace and harmony are desirable, then we must find information that is universal and unifying. This will solve the divisive problem of exclusivity.

While our earthen bound environments may be different, our cosmic identity remains the same. We have the same Mother and the same Father. In the last section, we wrote about the origin of living things on Earth. While everyone may not agree on the details, there is usually no trouble with understanding the Earth as our Mother. Because of the consensus, this is a unifying idea. Continuing with the same unifying theme, it should be simple to recognize who our Father is. We are referring to the Mother and Father of all living things on the planet. We are not limiting our discussion to the exclusive class of human beings as if we have some special, segregated covenant with God that makes us God's favorites or gives us dominion. The Father of bacteria is the same as the Father of humans. As a result of imposed religious dogma, it makes it difficult for many of us to recognize who our Father is. Our Mother Earth has a husband. Our Father is the Sun. He lives in the heavens. This reality is confusing for Christians because they have been taught the Heavenly Father is God. That is fiction. It is a false teaching. A little honesty would make it clear that we learned this from the slaver. We did not learn this from our ancestors or from God. Our Heavenly Father is the sun, but he is not God. This is what our ancestors taught on both sides of the Atlantic.

We sympathize with your confusion because our spiritual journey started with Christianity many years ago. From experience we know that you can get over it. In the U.S., Christianity is convenient but that does not make it correct. If you want to know truth, you are going to have to overcome the herding instinct and the emotional connection to the slaver's religious views. We are not talking about a few bad ideas. The invader did not bring us any truth, zero. If you do not have any trouble understanding what zero means, then let the slave teachings go. If you want to be filled with truth, empty your poisoned cup. In the last section, we were careful to offer an alternative explanation of who we are. We confined that discussion to water and land. Some readers may have even considered it to be divisive, although that was not our intent. Let us look at who we are on a cosmic level, which should be completely unifying. If we are made up of the Earth and the Sun, then we are Earth dust and stardust. That is one way to describe who we are. We are fire. We are lights just like our Father. We burn at nearly 100°F every day. We take it for granted; but when it is 100°F outside, we all consider this to be hot. We are a little piece of who are Father is.

The earthen part is more obvious. We are mostly water just like our Mother. We have a semi-solid surface. We are made up of the same minerals, etc. There are a lot of books on our relationship with our Mother Earth. For our discussion, it is sufficient to know that she must be loved and respected like all Mothers. This starts by fully understanding that she is alive. We may say we are aware of this, but our actions demonstrate that we are not. If we were, we would not be pumping out her oil. This is part of her life force. If it was not a life source, then it would not provide energy. It is the same with our Father. He is our source of energy and he is our life source. We do not understand the scripture that says honor your Mother and Father that your days may be long upon the Earth. At some point, we hope the masses will realize that draining our Mother of her life sources and minerals is suicidal, but correctable. If we destroy her, we destroy ourselves. We currently rape our Mother of anything we need to make ourselves more comfortable. This is madness. We have been told this for many years but we seem to be too far entrenched to actually do anything about it. If we realized the consequences of our actions, we would know the urgency of the moment. We will try to broaden our knowledge of our Mother and Father in an effort to help create a more sustainable world view.

Since many of us have been taught the Heavenly Father is God, it becomes difficult to reconcile the observance of the Sun as our Heavenly Father. When we say the Heavenly Father as God is fiction, this does not mean that God is fiction. It only means that God is something other than the Heavenly Father, although the omnipotent God has to include the Sun. Normally, when we talk about God, we are talking about the beginning. If we can identify the beginning of all living things, then we should be able to confidently call this beginning, God. Some people with far eastern spiritual training may say that there is no beginning. Since we are focused here on universal and unifying truths, we will not disagree. Let us preface our discussion by saying that if there is a beginning, we have found a liberating way to explain it. As mentioned, if there is a beginning, then we can legitimately call this God. We are moving our discussion from who we are to who God is. We think this will help us better understand who we are. At a minimum, it will make us less vulnerable to religious indoctrination. It will liberate us from an imaginary world of religious illusions and political expediency.

We are saying in no uncertain terms that the God of the Bible is imaginary and fiction. The Bible does not tell us who God is. Moses and/or the scribes of his time changed the concept of Heavenly Father from our tangible Sun to an imaginary concept of God which is never explained. The scribes wrote about attributes of God and where God is supposed to be, but not who God is. Knowledge of who God is had to be ignored in order to disconnect the Hebrews from Nature. Once disconnected, they could steal, kill and destroy indiscriminately and say their actions were sanctioned by God. This could be done because the God that they claim promised someone else's land to them does not exist. It is political make believe. Those wanting power and control make others believe through religion. It should not be hard for us to see since these beliefs were obviously forced on Black Americans. We were made to believe in Christianity. We were not learning from the Bible before we were invaded, enslaved and changed into slave thinkers. Europeans invaded America in the same way that Hebrews invaded Canaan. They also used the same excuse that their actions were condoned by God. Surely we can see that this is political and not spiritual.

Let's begin to clear up the confusion. People who have been oppressively indoctrinated with Christianity will likely be asking the question: if the Heavenly Father is not God, who is God? One thing we know for sure is that God cannot be a Father. So far, we have defined God as the beginning. There is more to it, but this is a good starting point. A Father is not the beginning of any living thing. We had some discussion on the seed, the egg as the beginning as opposed to roots. Well, the seed/egg comes from the Mother. Just because sea horse children hatch from the male sea horse's pouch does not mean the Father gave them life. The beginning is in the egg. The Mother put the eggs in his pouch. Some male birds sit on the eggs until they hatch, but the eggs still came from the Mother. There is undeniable proof in Nature that some living things do not have a Father at all. Some living things do not even have a male in the species. It appears the only thing we must have for life is a Mother. There are some creatures that have no gender. Bacteria, for example reproduces through binary fission. It has a direct Mother and Father relationship. The Earth and the Sun are its parents. Although it has no gender, it is still born of a Mother. Recall that this is the first child of Mother Earth. Some creatures have both genders. Some humans are born this way. Parents typically decide to remove one set of sexual organs. Still others can change gender. Frogs are an interesting group. Some frogs can change sexes so that the males become females in order to bear children and survive...because you must have a Mother to have a beginning.

In early 2008, it was reported that a hammerhead shark and a komodo dragon were able to give birth in the absence of a male. These are not female only species, but they were able to conceive and give birth without a male. These were true virgin births. We bring up the gender of various living things to make it clear that a Father is not the beginning of anything. The origin of all living things is the Mother. We generally understand God to be the Author of life, the source of life, the beginning of all living things. In any language and in any country, if we are talking about the beginning, it will be understood that we are referring to God. This assumes we are communicating with people who can conceptualize a beginning. In the final analysis, we find the beginning which we call God has to be a Mother. The beginning of all living things is a Mother. This is truth. This is not religion. For those with a concept of Father God, this is paradigm changing information. This necessitates a discussion about what truth is. We are not philosophers so we will offer a very simple explanation. It is important that we know how to determine whether a minister or priest is telling us the truth or leaning towards political ends. How do we know if something is true? Will our chosen Holy book show us the way?

Unfortunately, we have become vulnerably reliant on our favorite scripture to enable us to discern between truth and falsehoods. This begs the question: how did we determine what was true before there were books? What was God's word before there were scribes? We have mentioned that we should look to the universal laws in order to make us less vulnerable to following the herd into belief system bondage. Popular belief systems leave us unwittingly bound to hierarchal control and exploitation. Before we were disconnected from Nature by the slaver, it was clear that the Laws of God are the Laws of Nature. These are the laws that are universally reliable. Man did not write the Laws of Nature. God did. Since man is fallible, all scriptures have mistakes. No scriptures are the Laws of God. They may provide a good moral compass, but this is man's decision about what is good and bad. This is not from God. This is political or perhaps we can just say ethical. The more we understand about the Laws of Nature, the better we can discern if a scripture is political or spiritual. If our scripture does not measure up to the Laws of Nature, then who is the liar, God or man? Who is mistaken? Are the Laws of Nature incorrect because man wants to believe something written long ago is true?

Hopefully we can see how this approach will make us less credulous readers of scripture. We have heretofore been gullible because we have not taken the time to meditate or to delve into any independent thought.

Without independent thought, we follow the herd. The herd is accelerating its pace to world destruction. Your scripture may prophesy this as a certainty; but Mother Nature teaches us that survival is possible. Viruses are designed to self-destruct. Humans are designed to survive. Recall section 1. We have apparently misunderstood the nature of prophecy. Prophets are not divine soothsayers. They are clairvoyant in the sense that they know enough about the nature of things to be able to see beyond ordinary perception. Prophets are seers, not future predictors. Generally speaking, prophets warned that we are headed for a suicidal end if and only if we do not change our ways. We argue that it is possible for us to change our ways. We know this is possible because we know who we are and we know who God is in a way that is consistent with Nature and defensible. Among other things, God is the Author of possibility. If we come to know that we can survive rather than believing that we must die, it will constructively and positively change our world view. It will open up our world to further creativity and enlightenment. It will enable us to engage each other in dialogue about universal truths as opposed to religious beliefs.

This brings us to a crossroad as we try to navigate between truth and belief. This is not the exclusive domain of philosophers or metaphysicians. Everyday people are supposed to be able to recognize the Laws of Nature. For sustainability, this has to be the core of what we learn as we are herded through the school buildings and temples every week. Based on our logic thus far, we show that we can determine what is true by measuring it against the Laws of Nature. We often measure things against our scriptural beliefs. These scriptures have been written by men who may have politically charged motivations. The interpretations of these men are not as reliable as interpretations of the Laws of Nature. Religious views are not universal, nor are they unifying. The Laws of Nature, on the other hand, can liberate us from divisive religious differences as we learn to respect and appreciate our natural differences. Years ago, religious leaders led the masses away from a connectedness with Nature. It was not just with Hebrews. Christianity, for example, violently displaced a connectedness with Nature in Europe and everywhere else it spread. We have not forgotten the crusades and the inquisitions that preceded colonialism and slavery. Religious men wanted to take control away from God. They wanted the power to control men and the world themselves. Their power hungry nature led them to believe they had the power to control

Nature and everything in it. This extreme case of hubris is a sad and suicidal misjudgment. Let's see if we can help to correct it.

CHAPTER 16

FEMININE DESCRIPTIONS OF GOD

THE invader has successfully supplanted a suicidal belief system into our normal cultural practice. Now, this has become our comfort zone. We have internalized faith in beliefs that bind us to self-destructive behavior patterns. Liberation from beliefs of bondage opens our lives to paths of wisdom, truth and freedom. At this point, we have loosely defined truth as those things we can validate using the laws of Nature. We will loosely define beliefs as those things we want to be true. We really do not know if they are true. We do not necessarily have any tangible, supporting evidence. But since we want them to be true and it makes us comfortable, we put these things in a category called belief. The problem is that we erroneously equate our beliefs with truth. The Virgin Mother story is one such belief. We will try to show the truth that undergirds the symbolism in the story toward an effort to build a bridge to understanding who God is. In keeping with our main idea of liberation, we will take a non-patriarchal approach. We will start with three feminine aspects of who God is. Then we will proceed with three androgynous aspects.

We have already discussed the Laws of Nature being the laws of God. Following this logic, God must be the author of the Laws of Nature, or at least the functioning embodiment of the Laws of Nature. We typically call this Mother Nature. If Mother Nature is not God, who is? We don't have to believe that Mother Nature is God, we experience it. This is the basis of Animism. It is also very close to what we were learning before we were invaded, enslaved and forced to learn the slaver's religious views. One of the fundamental tenets of Animism is that everything is alive and must be respected. This is a Law of Nature. Our understanding of Mother Nature need not be limited to the Earth, so let us set up a discussion of the origin of the cosmos.

For those of you who have seen the Zeitgeist movie, you may already be familiar with some of the things we are about to mention. We have been teaching this for almost 15 years, so we did not get it from the Zeitgeist movie but it makes it easier to explain now that there is other information readily available. Near the beginning of this docu-movie, the narrator mentions that he cannot tell you who God is, but he can show you who God is not. He essentially points to the story of Yoshua (Jesus) as a hoax because there are so many similar stories that precede it. This is perfectly logical and we are not going to subtract from it. We are going to add to it. The story of Jesus is mythology, but that is okay. The square root of negative one is also imaginary. This does not preclude us from having valid uses for it, however, in the complex number system. This illustrates our approach. When we take the square root of negative one, we get an imaginary number. As long as we stick with the Laws of Nature, which in this case is mathematics, this is okay. When we square this imaginary number, we get back to negative one, which is a real number. It is not a natural number, but it is a real number. Likewise, we can take the mythological story of the human Virgin Mother, stay with the Laws of Nature and come back to an important reality.

One of the first liberating things to realize is that the story of Mary and Jesus is not the only Virgin Mother story around. Afrocentric researchers are well aware of this. A basic study of Egyptian history reveals the story of Isis, the Virgin Mother. This story was literally written in stone more than 2,000 years before Mary and Jesus. This information alone has liberated many from a Christian based belief system. Consider the dilemma we are faced with. We cannot see our God as a copy cat storyteller. That is not acceptable. Logically, the earlier story would more likely be true if one of the stories were true. Alternatively, they could both be false. What did not make sense was for the story of Isis to be false and the story of Mary to be true. So, we kept seeking truth and meditating. Eventually, the introspective journey brought us back to the Americas where we found Bloodwoman, the Virgin Mother in Mexico. This story was also thousands of years older than the Hebrew story. There was a direct link between the Hebrew story and the Egyptian story. It was less clear as to why a very similar story existed on the other side of the Atlantic in an entirely different hemisphere. Since these were different ecological regions, there must have been some cosmic reason behind these similarities.

An important thing to note about the similarities is that the Virgin Mother always had a male child. This child was always a light, the Enlightened One. The Virgin Mother story also existed in India. The Hopi in the American southwest also have a Virgin Mother story. We are not trying to give an exhaustive list of these stories. Suffice it to know that the Virgin Mother story existed all over the world long before Mary and Jesus. This was literally written in stone on different continents, so it is evidence that cannot be refuted. This should take a little wind out of the sails of those who thought there was some kind of special authenticity with the Christian story the slaver brought. Although Yoshua (Jesus) is the latest story, this does not necessarily mean that it is a copy. The Hebrews may have been seeing the same thing that much of the world was seeing. Since human virgins cannot give birth to male children, there must be more to the story than what we have been taught. A human virgin could possibly give birth, but without any male contribution to the gene pool, the child could only be a clone of herself. It could only be a female child. The Virgin Mother giving birth to a male child, who is a light to the world, is an important part of the story. In the American version of the story, the Virgin Mother has twins, two lights. This is an important distinction as well which we will cover later.

Let's consider how this relates to who God is. In order to find out who God is, we can start where we are and go backward. We know that we came from our Mother. She comes from her Mother and so on. Even our Father comes from his Mother. We took this beyond the selfish human realm and looked at frogs, birds, bacteria and sea horses. We even looked at some non-human virgin births involving the hammerhead shark and the Komodo dragon. We found that all living things come from a Mother. Therefore, the Mother has to be the beginning. We call God the beginning. God must logically be a Mother. Based on the Laws of Nature, God cannot be a father. We showed that pastoral people and patriarchal people typically see God as a Father. Religiously, this is fine because it may be consistent with survival in their ecological conditions. Spiritually, however, this is not consistent with the Laws of Nature. Our beginning, in whatever way we define it, is from a Mother. Our beginning on the Earth is from a Mother. The beginning of the cosmos is also a Mother. What was there in the cosmos in the beginning?

Before the beginning, there was nothing. There was only the darkness. We can observe stars being born and we know they have a finite life span. So, in the beginning and in the end, there is only darkness. The only everlasting substance is the darkness. It is nothingness and it is all possibility at the same time. There are some things we can say about this darkness.

We can say fertility existed in the darkness because at some point living things came to be. Living things are born, not created. This is a great misconception from the Bible. Once we change living things to being created rather than born, then we can change God into being a dominant male rather than a Mother. For example, a house is created from living material that already exists. A pot is created on a potter's wheel from live clay. Our discussion of the beginning has to do with the birth of living material, not merely the re-fashioning of pre-existing structures. A child is not fashioned as a creation. A child is born of a Mother. This gives us some background for our second description of who God is. The beginning whom we call God is the Fertile Darkness, who exists beyond time. More simply, God is the Fertile Darkness. This is our second feminine description of who God is. God, as the Beginning, cannot be a male in the real world. This can only exist in the world of belief. We have introduced how God is Mother Nature and how God is the Fertile Darkness. Let's continue with the idea of God as a Mother. The Fertile Darkness is a Mother. This is before the beginning. This is before time existed. Only the Mother existed. We know that living things were born somehow. How did it happen? If the Mother was there all alone, who was there to impregnate her? The answer is no one. This was before the yin and yang. This was before the hero twins.

Since there was no one there to impregnate her, the Mother in the beginning had to be a Virgin. The darkness was fertile. The Virgin modified herself and gave birth to light. But this was not a clone of herself. He was a male child. He was the first star, the first light. He was the enlightened One. From the Zero came forth the One. From nothing came something. The Virgin Mother gave birth to a male child like our Heavenly Father, the Sun. The male child was the bringer of light. He was to enlighten the world. He was the first Sun. This was the dawn of life. This was truly the Immaculate Conception. This concept is not unlike the singularity in the Big Bang Theory. It is a bridge between our ancestral teachings and modern science. The Virgin Mother is our third description of who God is. From a multi-dimensional perspective, it becomes clear that God is the Virgin Mother in our stories who gave birth to light symbolized by the Enlightened One. The Virgin Mother stories have been passed down to us as myths, but they survive to tell us the story of our Beginning. We notice that all of the Virgin Mothers in the stories gave birth to a male child who is also a light. The Virgin Mother story has no literal connection to Jesus of Nazareth. The Virgin Mother story is a story of how light as life was immaculately conceived from darkness, a story of how something arose from nothing.

So far, we have introduced that God is Mother Nature, God is the Fertile Darkness and God is the Virgin Mother. These are the three feminine aspects of who God is. Let's turn our attention to some other ways of describing who God is as we free ourselves of religious indoctrination. The Hebrews told us they were God's favorites and they used this self-proclaimed superiority to invade and destroy other people. The reality is that they are not God's favorites. Humans are not God's favorites. Once we understand that God is not a bad parent who chooses favorites as the Hebrews proposed, then we become free to realize that God is the Life Force in all living things. We are saying that God is not just the Life Force in Hebrews. God is not just the Life Force in human beings. God is the collective Life Force in all ling things, simultaneously. God is not a superior in a far away kingdom of perfection making decisions about who has been good or bad like Santa Claus. As we discussed about the diagram of the cross within the circle, God is in the center of your being. God is not at the top and the Devil is not at the bottom. Incidentally, this is also in the Bible in the book of Luke: Chapter 17:21. The Bible says "…the Kingdom of God is within you." Notice this has nothing to do with being Supreme, Superior or Hierarchal. These are not attributes of God. These are flaws in man. These are the flaws that cause wars and unnecessary suffering because people reject domination.

Our fourth description of God is that God is the Life Force in all living things. There is no hierarchy in this description. It becomes an inside-outside world rather than a top and bottom world. It would be insightful to envision something more like concentric circles to illustrate our relationship with God and other living things. So, let's consider the core of who we are and what is emanating from there. We have demonstrated that we are bits of the Earth and bits of the Sun as well as bits of the Fertile Darkness. We are particles of the spiritual magic that keeps us alive. We know this simply because we have life. God is life. Since we are living, we share some scaled down characteristics of the original Life Force. This relates to our survival and the spiritual depth of who we are because of our relationship with our children. We can be confident that we are God's children. God lives in all of us at the same time. Understanding how God lives in more than one form helps us to see how we can live in more than one form at the same time. We cannot be omnipresent by living in all things at the same time; but we can live in many forms simultaneously. As with the nature of God, the Sun and the Earth, it is through our children that we are able to extend into several life forms.

Recall that the Fertile Darkness modified herself and became the Light. The Earth modified herself and eventually became a human. The human Mother also modifies herself and becomes another, often more than one new entity. When the Mother conceives a child, the child is another form of the Mother. The Mother's identity is not lost. Although combined with the genes of a man, she is fully present in her child. Similar to the Omni-present nature of God, the human Mother lives in more than one form at the same time. If the Mother has 15 children, then the Mother lives in 16 forms simultaneously. We are not excluding Fatherhood in this discussion. The same is true for the male. The sperm is also the entire male. It is not just a part. When the sperm goes into the egg, if it conceives, then that male remains alive. We know that the entire male is there because the child can be made up of any of his genes. In combination with the Mother's genes, he is transformed into a new entity. If a man has 20 children, then he lives in 21 forms simultaneously. We share continuity with our parents and children that transcend one lifespan. One unambiguous way to explain everlasting life is to think of the depth of life we have in our children. When we perish, it is clear that the part of us that remains living is our children.

If we understood our relationship to our children in this context, it would point us in the direction of sustainability. In order to live forever, we have to take care of our environment and our children. When we see the world in this way, it does not seem farfetched that Indigenous Americans would consider seven generations in the future before making major ecological decisions. We have to understand the depth of who we are. We need to realize how we are connected to our ancestors and our children. Our beginning is in our ancestors. Our everlasting life is in our children. Understanding the world in this way helps to steer us in a direction of learning from history and leaving more resources for our children rather than depleting them. When we are taught that we have an individual experience with everlasting life, we are not provided with the incentive to make sure our children survive. Nor are we provided with evidence of anything everlasting. We just want to make sure that we make it into heaven. This leaves us vulnerable to being spiritually divided, manipulated and conquered. It breaks the spiritual continuity between parents and children. The parents can sneak off to heaven, while the unruly children are damned to hell. As we realize that our children are our everlasting life, we can begin to repair the broken spiritual connection with our children. Our actions for the future become constructive rather than destructive. If we really understood our future as our children here on Earth, we would not destroy the world in the way that we do. We accept the destruction because we are taught that it is inevitable and we can be granted a separate everlasting experience in an imaginary heaven.

Some readers may be wondering about everlasting life for those who have no children. Allow us to recapitulate before addressing this issue. We mentioned that one of the problems with an individual experience with everlasting life is that we disconnect from our children and our environment. If our living is unhealthy and destructive to the environment, we may experience the same in death. When we perish, our physical bodies return to the Earth. If the Earth is damaged, then this is the condition to which we return. If She is healthy, then we return to a healthy condition. We cannot escape accountability whether we have children or not. One of the things that helps put the individual experience in perspective for those without children is the understanding of a light year. If a star is 10,000 light years away, we will not see the light until 10,000 years after the star emits it. During this time, the star may have already perished. We will still see the light for thousands of years after the star has perished. About 10,000 years after the star perishes, we will not see that star anymore. But any entities 20,000 light years on the other side of us will still see that star's light for another 20,000 years.

Since we are also lights, this applies to our bits of stardust also. Our light will essentially shine forever through space and time. Even after a star collapses into a black hole; or after a human collapses into the black Earth, the light will still shine in space to those far away. Even if we don't have children, our light still shines forever. So, everlasting life is a part of who we are. We don't have to follow an invading culture's belief system to be granted everlasting life. The invader seems to hold all of the rights and privileges of our humanity, to include our spiritual connection to God. If we love ourselves and our children, we must use our religious venues to begin to quickly correct this problem. In an open-ended scenario of everlasting life through our children, there is incentive to leave the world in a better place. In a scenario of individual gain and a pre-ordained destructive end, there is no incentive to leave the world in a better place. The seeds of our destruction are in our spiritual world view. Practicing the slaver's religions keep us bound to the slaver's spirituality and thus bound to his destructiveness.

Regardless of what religion we believe in, our best chance at survival and everlasting life is to work toward a sustainable world view. The world view we are sharing with you is historical, sustainable and pragmatic. What we are sharing about spirituality is not an abstract theory without practical purposes. We are combining the ingredients of knowledge to show us a clear path to longevity. The following triangle illustrates this idea:

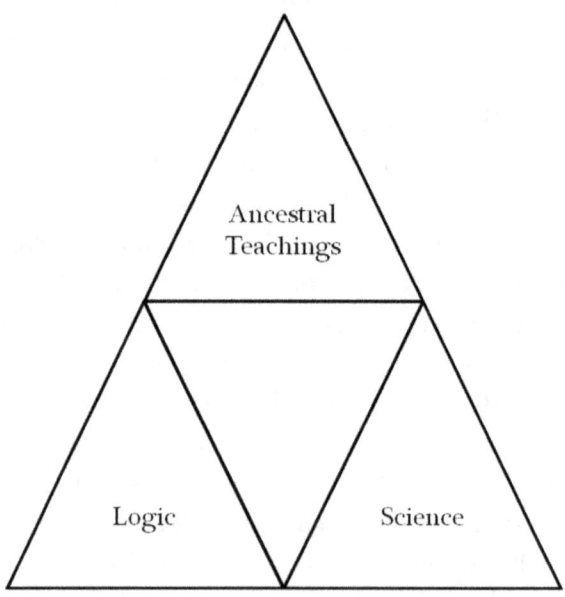

As shown in our triangle, we combine our ancestral teachings, logic and science to help us understand the past, present and future. When our experiences are narrated for us by the oppressor who controls our education, we often see triangles like pyramids and immediately think in terms of hierarchy. Just as with the cross in the circle, there is no hierarchal order to the triangle described above. Use of this triangle helps to take away many of our vulnerabilities.

Earlier we wrote about filtering our information through the laws of Nature to make sure that we have a solid spiritual foundation. Filtering through the triangle ensures that we have a solid stem for growth to blossom. Using the tools of the triangle and the cross within the circle, we should be able to find our way out of the religious box. Spirituality is not edifying if it cannot get us out of the box. What we are sharing about our ancestral spirituality does not leave us trapped and defenseless against oppression. The true spiritual self has vitality. It will not remain dominated and doomed to destruction. The good news is not that Jesus came to wash away our sins. This is completely empty rhetoric as part of a boxed in belief system. It does nothing to free our minds, bodies or spirits. The good news is that we don't have to be dominated by a foreign virus forever because God, as the spirituality within us, is more powerful than the invader's aggression and disease. The best fitting word in English to describe the spirituality of the blacks around the Atlantic is Animism. This spiritual concept is broad enough to enable us to understand who we are, where we are and what is going on. We can safely use this to describe an Atlantic view of spirituality without getting boxed in and dogmatic. Animism sees the world as simultaneously diverse and integrated.

The key has always been to recognize balance, to resonate harmoniously with the ebb and flow of Nature. For example, populations become large and populations become small. Civilizations grow large and civilizations fall. These cultural and collective memories become a part of our re-told legends (religions). The memories are typically embellished with codes of conduct that are designed to circumvent known reasons for the collapse of civilizations, populations and individuals. When we keep these stories alive, we increase our survivability. When a foreign culture comes in like a virus to replace our knowledge of Nature and harmony, then obviously our survivability is greatly reduced. We can return to being fully human if we return to understanding our connectedness to God and each other. All we have to do is genuinely want to survive in the long term. We have to be farsighted enough to be able to see the need for unity and see the great danger in depending on the oppressor for our spiritual and physical sustenance.

Being dependent on the oppressor's view of God brings us back to the aggression of the bishop on the chess board. The strategy of this seemingly innocent war game is maliciously used to crush our spirits in the real world. The attack of the bishop on the chess board is representative of millions of Black Americans reduced to the belief systems of those who enslaved us. Our spirituality is off the board in the game of life as a result of biological warfare with its consequent fear and neglect. It is time for a true revival of our own spiritual paths. We need not wonder why we are not overcoming slavery. If we truly want to survive as individuals and as a group, then we will have to get our minds, bodies and spirits in the game.

For those unfamiliar with the chess game, each player is endowed with two bishops whom are very mobile and useful in playing to win. It should be obvious that in real life, we do not have either of our bishops on the board and we are losing very badly. Christianity and Islam are inadequate replacements for our own spirituality represented by the bishop. In order to have our bishops on the board, we must embrace our ancestral spirituality and embrace Mother Nature's rules. As a result of losing the spiritual battle, we are losing our life force. We are losing our vitality and ability to resist. We are losing the wherewithal to survive. This means that the survival of our children is in jeopardy. In order to stop genocide, we must think more clearly about our direction. When this house of cards comes crashing down, it may completely annihilate the people at the bottom, which are black people. To correct this problem, we have to change directions spiritually, mentally and politically. We have to stop allowing the dominant culture to play the same tricks on every generation. Spiritual liberation will enable us to anticipate the tricks and overcome them.

Some examples are as follows. The idea that Jesus made us free is a trick. The idea that Abraham Lincoln made us free is a trick. The idea that Dr. Martin Luther King, Jr. made us free is a trick. The idea the Barak Obama makes us free is a trick. The belief that wealthy blacks can sell us out and live large while the rest of black people perish is also a trick. The oppressor is known to use the elite to sell our people out and then dispose of them also. We cannot see these tricks because we follow the herd like spiritual zombies with our eyes covered over by destructive belief systems. We have great spiritual power within us if we are willing to unveil it so that we can use it strategically and constructively for spiritual and physical survival. At this time, our spiritual power remains locked behind walls of hierarchy and patriarchy, behind walls of mis-education and political deceitfulness, behind walls of economic marginalization. We have to get our own Shaman on the board and get the oppressor's bishops out of our territory. Recall that these include primarily Judaism, Christianity and Islam. We are just trying to expose the deception and shed light on the power of the life force within us that we call God. From this context of spiritual revival, let's move forward and build on the story of the Virgin Mother as the Author of life.

The process of reviving our spirituality means retelling our stories. It means interpreting them in ways that are consistent with our pre-invasion past. We want to use the Virgin Mother story to help build a bridge to a better understanding of ourselves and our world. As previously mentioned, the Indigenous American stories have an additional insight. The Virgin Mother on the west side of the Atlantic Ocean has twins. From one perspective on Earth, the twins are analogous to the Sun and the Moon. From a cosmic perspective, there are other inferences. In the eastern case of only one light (enlightened One) emerging from the darkness, we cannot yet have the beginning of time. We measure time as the movement of one object in relation to another. If we only have one object, then we cannot measure time. Measuring time requires at least two entities. Darkness is not an entity. Darkness is.

In the Native American case, the Virgin Mother, the Fertile Darkness gives birth to twins. This story gives us two lights. Since we can measure the movement of one light in relation to another, the Virgin birth of twins can include a representation of the beginning of time. This version of the birth of life includes the birth of time as well as yin and yang, random and deterministic, etc. Harmony, sharing, balance and polar opposites are inferred by the twins of the western Virgin Mother. This is a spiritual view that breaks down patriarchy because the dominant male architecture is not supported. The most important and practical implication, however, is sharing. Individualism is balanced with the responsibility of sharing. Competition is balanced with cooperation. There is no first one in this unadulterated view of the world. There is no apex or top spot. Not surprisingly, the resulting structure we end up with is like a flat topped pyramid where power is shared as symbolized by the twins.

CHAPTER 17

ANDROGYNOUS DESCRIPTIONS OF GOD

THROUGHOUT this discussion of liberating spirituality, we are confirming the idea of a monotheistic beginning. We have referred to this beginning as the Virgin Mother, the Fertile Darkness and Mother Nature. This is, in a sense, before the beginning. So, without contradiction, we are also discussing multiple firsts, multiple lights born from the Darkness. Notice this relates to the previous section on multiple firsts on Earth. Our relationship to our singular origin is not well described by concepts of 'first' or 'apex'. The relationship is not hierarchal in time (as a first) or space (as a top). While difficult to explain in English, there is a Mayan word that captures this concept very well. In the Mayan language, the name Hunab Ku means One Giver of Movement and Measure. Notice this is another non-hierarchal name of God and it is our fifth description of who God is. As narrated by invaders, we learn of a Mayan pantheon of gods assumed to be evidence of polytheism. The name Hunab Ku implies something different. The invader often uses polytheism to show people as primitive and inferior. From a more liberating perspective, the first syllable in Hunab Ku means one. The implication is monotheism. The second part of the meaning of Hunab Ku is Giver. This giving is our endowment at birth so far in our discussion of the Mother as the beginning.

So, Giver in this context is not exactly synonymous with Creator. Looking at the latter part of our word, we find that our endowments of movement and measure can also be termed energy and form. From the formless darkness of possibility, the Mother gave birth to energy and form. These are not to be confused with the twin lights born of the darkness. Each twin has energy and form. Understand that space and time are connected through Movement and Measure. When something moves against the background of something else, we measure the change and call it time. Putting it all together, we find that Hunab Ku is monotheistic and relates to the singularity in the beginning in a way that does not define a Supreme just to define an origin. This is an important distinction for our future, particularly if we envision a more equitable, non-hierarchal society. An understanding of the cosmic beginning as we have described is a bridge for those who want to transcend the spiritual inferiority complex. The spiritual deception of a patriarchal and hierarchal belief system has been devastating. The historically proven solution to solving the long term problems of slavery and oppression is to begin with embracing our ancestral spirituality. This will enable us to create a more sustainable plan of survival including a more equitable and harmonious social order.

Dr. White taught that Mother Nature favors the home team. We find this to be true, which means that for the long term, we must learn Indigenous American spirituality if we intend to remain here. This brings us back to understanding who we are, where we are and what is going on. We must stop passing down our post-slavery spirituality which perpetuates the slavery of our children. This is to remain connected to an identity crisis, which leaves us vulnerable to continued abuse. We can reverse the process of slavery by liberating our spirits. Theological liberation provides a foundation for emotional and mental liberation which provides for physical liberation. As we begin to recognize that Nature provides us with the rules of life and survival, we can create a sustainable foundation and begin to truly rise from the bottomless pit. Oftentimes, when people become politically free, they become oppressors themselves because all that they know is this dichotomous way of life; and we have been inculcated with the idea that this is the best way to order society. We suggest that there is a healthier and more sustainable path to liberation, which is not the same as freedom. Liberation will lead to freedom, but freedom may not lead to liberation. Liberated people will not behave like their oppressors. Liberated people will not practice the invader's religion nor sing his songs. Dr. White taught us that a robin does not teach its young a blue jay song.

There may be up to five species of birds living in one tree. What does this teach us about peace and unity? In the absence of domination unity can occur. We have learned from Middle Eastern religions that God is a dominant male being. This is quite opposite the real world and, as a result, creates chaos rather than harmony. Disorderly dominance and greed are made to look like order and wisdom. Looking back at our fourth description of who God is, we find that God is the collective life force in all living things. This implies that the Supreme Being or Supreme Power is in the collective force of unity. In contrast to God as a dominator to justify political corruption, God is Unity exemplified by the birds in the trees. Keep in mind the predator-prey relationship is a different kind of unity. This has undeniably been the relationship between invading Europeans and Black Americans. Of course, integration destroys the order which causes both the prey and the predator to perish. The aggression of America's invader has been extreme. Restoring order will require extreme measures of defense on the part of the unnatural prey. Unity can be achieved when the defense matches the aggression because we are not really prey and will not survive if we do not achieve better balance. Since God as Unity is a function of God as Life Force, we are not treating this as a separate description.

We would like to offer one final description of who God is. This is our sixth description. Again we will use a Mayan concept since most of our own language has been destroyed and English is inadequate. This is a dual concept described as Heart of Sky, Heart of Earth. There can be no supremacy, favoritism or dominance associated with this term. We think it could also be interpreted as Life of Sky/Earth. It is an extension of God as the Life Force because it encompasses the life force of the sky and the life force of the earth. The Mayans recognized the human heart as a symbol of the life force of human beings. Our heart is a four chambered life force like the four chambers of our cross within the circle diagram. It symbolizes the Life Force, but also the Origin. This relates back to Hunab Ku. The Measure of our being can be found in our blood. The Movement of our being is found in our respiration. Heart of Sky/Earth includes everything. The Life Force lends itself to a discussion of Unity. Heart of Sky/Earth, with implications of all inclusiveness, lends itself to a discussion of Omnipotence. Allow us to build some framework for this idea using three binary concepts. A spiritually liberated mind set will enable us to discern between the following three pairs: constructive and destructive, truth and belief as well as political and spiritual.

If we view our social world with a healthy dose of criticism, we find that much of what we think is advancement is actually primitive. Much of what we think is constructive development is actually destructive and unsustainable. Processes that work against Nature are destructive. Construction only occurs when processes are followed that resonate in harmony with Nature. This provides a way to categorize productive actions without being confined to the opinionated moral compass of good and evil. For example, two of our major destructive issues on the planet are oil production and compound interest. In a modern twisted world, these are the very pillars of development. We are taught these are used for construction. When we consider many costs unaccounted for, we realize we are shortening our days. Oil and compound interest are destructive. Constructive and destructive are closely related to good and evil. These concepts are very subjective, but it is useful to see where they fit in with understanding who God is.

If we know that God is Omnipotent, then good and evil must both be a part of who God is. In this explanation, we are defining Omnipotent as all inclusive rather than all powerful. If God is Omnipotent and Omnipresent, then there can be nothing outside of the personhood of God. Being confined to the good and evil paradigm leaves us vulnerable to emotional manipulation such as Bush's axis of evil in the Middle East. Discard this ideology altogether and a cleaner view of truth can emerge. The new question becomes, which culture is more constructive or less destructive? Considering Bush's axis of evil, at the end of the day, who is terrorizing who? There are no Muslims terrorizing in the U.S., but the U.S. is murdering Muslims in their home country on a daily basis. The destructiveness of the U.S. is clear. This behavior is associated with evil, so it becomes clear where the axis of evil is if we define it as destructiveness. It is perpetrated not only against Black Americans, Africans and others, but against Arabs as well. We allow this kind of violence to go unchecked largely because of our belief system, hence the need for liberation theology. We think the constructive vs. destructive framework helps liberate us from the moral misjudgments of good and evil.

Our second pair of ideas is belief and truth. Note that belief is not truth and faith is not reality. Belief and faith cannot make us free. Although belief and faith may make us feel better about satisfying a sense of religious awareness, they actually increase our vulnerability to manipulation. We do not have to go any further than the Bible to describe the kind of freedom that truth should provide. We can measure the Emancipation Proclamation with the same political independence as the Hebrews freedom from Egypt. Obviously, there is no truth in this document since it did not make us free like the children of Israel. According to the Bible, it is truth that makes us free. In reality, belief and faith make us vulnerable. When we begin to see that self-preservation must include freedom from all forms of Eurocentric domination, then it will become clear that we must start telling our children the truth. The truth is that Jesus is not our ancestor and neither is Muhammad. The truth is that Abraham Lincoln did not free any black people anywhere. Hebrew freedom did not leave them working for the Egyptians; yet we still work for the slaver. The same time and energy we spend on teaching our children the insulting lies of the oppressor, we could spend telling them the truth. We could teach them strategies to solve the problem of slavery, since it remains unresolved. One hundred more years of extreme terrorism and forty years of integration have not solved the problem of slavery. We have been in denial about this for quite some time because of a belief system that locks us into subordination regardless of a numerous name changes. We can call our condition slavery, freedom, oppression or whatever. The result is the same. We remain violently subordinated.

In order to emancipate ourselves from a destructively imposed belief system, a paradigm shift is required. This brings us to our third pair of ideas to discuss which is politics and spirituality. We have to cultivate awareness in which we can discern between political and spiritual posturing, whether it is written or spoken. Making a spiritual connection to our ancestors in this land will enable us to make the paradigm shift. We just have to learn to follow the paths of Nature as opposed to the paths of fiat money. Making a connection with the Indigenous American spirit will enable us to emerge from being bound to self-destructive belief systems. Specifically, the system we are boxed into also has a four-sided interpretation. Christianity, as taught by slavers to Black Americans, is a Eurocentric Hebrew Patriarchal Hierarchy. This is not a neatly fitting description, however, because so much of Christian scripture are actually the teachings of Paul.

One way to sharpen our discernment is to realize that anytime dominance comes into the picture, we know the teachings are political and not spiritual. Anytime teachings go against the Laws of Nature, this is political and not spiritual. When we are left with ideas that we cannot validate using our triangle of ancestral teachings, logic and science, we are probably being misled as political pawns as opposed to being spiritual players. When we are asked to believe or have faith, we are probably being set up politically rather than being edified spiritually. The oppressor's aggression is political and destructively spiritual. Our defensive solution must also be spiritual. If our movement is truly spiritual, it will lead to political independence just as it has historically done for other oppressed people. It is important to realize that we are not just dealing with a social mess that can be corrected with social change. We are still spiritual slaves. Mind, body and spirit must be liberated together.

We cannot just change a few laws and think the problem is solved. This is still part of the gradualism that M.L.K. Jr. spoke about. We cannot just amend the rules. We have to make our own rules from the ground up. As it has been said, we cannot make chicken soup out of chicken poop. We cannot make a political system that works for Black Americans out of a slave system that continues to this day. We have to rebuild our processes from dialogue and from scratch. The only reparations that make sense for Black Americans are to repair what was broken. As the bishop advanced on the chess board across the Atlantic, the western connection to God has been broken. Our political sovereignty was broken. Our linguistic connections and land connections have been broken. Can the oppressor repair these things? We think not. We definitely cannot begin to repair any of the damage with fiat money from a bankrupt country. This is insulting at best. In order for healing to occur, we have to rebuild our spiritual foundation in the same way that our bodies heal themselves. As previously mentioned, we have to recognize foreign spirituality, neutralize its effect, expel it and remember the invasion. Recognition of the healing process will enable us to organize with defenses against political corruption. Transparency and accountability are a natural part of spiritual systems that are developed from the Laws of Nature.

In contrast to spirituality, politics is used to control our herding instinct and thus control the masses. Our spirituality should enable us to see beyond political tricks. Our spirituality makes it clear that we have a responsibility to God and our children to become politically free of foreign domination. What kind of spirituality are we following that encourages us to fight for civil rights, spin in circles and remain slaves at the end of the day? This is obviously slave religion and not spiritual at all. We don't recognize the trickery involved in politics because our imposed religion does not equip us with what we need to be able to see beyond the veil of the herding masses. As we understand that spirituality is holistic, we may begin to see more clearly that our spiritual lives cannot be separated from our political lives. The so-called separation of church and state is a trick. The idea that invading Europeans fought for religious freedom is also a trick, or more like a blatant lie. The same invaders murdered Native people for practicing the ghost dance. This is how serious the oppressor is about keeping us from connecting to our true spirituality. Still to this day we do not hold Christians accountable for continuous murder of political foes. Religious murder in the new Millennium is no different from the religious murder in the early chapters of the Bible. We are still having trouble with clear discernment between politics and spirituality.

One criterion by which we can measure whether a church or mosque is political or spiritual is by the quality of its food production. As we lose the ability to feed ourselves, we also lose much of our spiritual connection and the ability to keep our young males from herding to prison. Hopefully at this point in our discussion, we understand our spiritual connection to the land and our food supply. Civilization begins with astronomy and agriculture. It is followed by religious practices designed to keep us in harmony with our pre-agricultural (original) paths and cycles. This is an integral part of who we are. Our original connection to God is always there as a guidepost. For example, many people in the U.S. have lost a sense of what human food is, especially among the young people. Originally, humans had no fire and therefore ate no cooked foods. This just about eliminates meat as a human food. It is a human adaptation but not a human food. Cow milk is obviously not human food. It is cow food. We took this little tangent just to demonstrate how to use our original connection to God as a guidepost when we have been misled.

Creating an external and internal environment conducive to spiritual learning is important to liberation theology. Making sure people have adequate local food is one of the most spiritual undertakings one can be involved with. There are many books on our spiritual connection to food, so we won't belabor this point. In the final analysis, every church or temple should be built in harmony with its environment and have a farm that can feed its parishioners along with water rights to accompany operations. The operations can be run by whoever in the community is unemployed which should help reduce the rate of incarceration. The idea we are trying to convey is that our survival in the U. S. begins with local food production. It is not wise to wait until we are starving to start working on this project. While politicians intend to starve us into submission, our spirituality teaches us to never give up local food production. For Black Americans, a church or mosque should not be allowed to exist if it cannot feed the people as a first priority. Spirituality is not separate from the physical world.

We have been very critical of Christianity, not only because it is the slaving belief system in the U.S. but also because it has had such a malevolent past. While we know the militant evangelism has not been benign, the misrepresented message of love has also been malignant. Christians did not bring love to the Americas in reality. They brought genocide. Christianity has been used as a part of the genocidal strategy just as the bishop is used strategically on the chess board. The problem for us moving forward is that in addition to having poor religious framework, the black church is built on a foundation of slavery. We have to rebuild from the ground up and from the cosmos down, simultaneously. We start with investigating our origins and finding out who we are. We have to follow the rules of Nature on this journey so as not to become boxed in, confused and misled. Then we can teach our 'Mother Nature guided' direction to our children as opposed to indoctrinating them with the oppressor's religious views.

There are five things in particular that we hope you will take away from this section on spirituality. First, we hope to have given a useful description of part of our inner and outer reality. Second, we trust that an opening to alternative views will take away our vulnerability to trickery. Third, we find that spiritual development complements our intellectual development. Fourth, Nature based views reconnect us with the environment that supports us. Fifth, this promotes awareness of and responsibility for the larger self. As we become more enlightened, the darkness will be forced away. Just like turning on the light in the bedroom forces out the darkness. This is very similar to the path in Buddhism of the cessation of suffering.

In terms of our origins, we discussed three descriptions of our life source and three descriptions of our life force. The life sources were the Virgin Mother, Fertile Darkness and Hunab Ku. The life forces were Mother Nature, Life Force in all living things and Heart of Sky/Earth. We corrected the Patriarchal God problem by explaining the Cosmic Mother, Earth Mother and Human Mother as one continuous thread of life. By all means, investigate these ideas. These truths will be found to be legitimate and necessary to teach our children and grandchildren so that they will not be spiritual slaves forever. Rich slave or poor slave, either way the path leads to a genocidal end. But time will be our friend if we decide to let a little light in. If we pull together based on our ancestral spirituality in the Americas, we can win.

Part 4

Epilogue

"To the degree that we establish a nation, our people will be stronger."[18]

C.L.R. James

Chapter 18

Invasion and Healing

IN the process of invasion, the military, missionary and corporation come to steal, kill and destroy. The invasions are made possible by taxes, consumers and banks. Typically, the hospitals, food supply and schools are directly or indirectly taken over by the foreign invading force. Laws are forced on the victims to protect the foreigner while maintaining disorder, disorientation and distrust among the victims. This is the one, two, three of invasion, takeover and dominate. Invasions infiltrate the body, land and culture. The good news is that there are known ways of stopping and reversing the process of invasion.

In the U.S., Natives, Africans and migrating Mexicans have all been invaded. In the process of healing, it will be necessary for us to dialogue and strategize so that we can implement specific plans to advance the process of healing ourselves, our land and our Atlantic culture. We are all familiar with the divide and conquer approach of the invader. Healing will require solidarity. This involves the creation of some common organizations directed towards solving some of the specific problems of the one, two three invasions.

Equally as important as the laws of the invasion are the works of the missionary previously discussed. Early in the process of healing, it is necessary to cleanse the spirit, to cleanse the mind of an invasive and destructive belief system. This is the simplest and most powerful way to begin overcoming oppression because there are pre-existing venues for organization and motivation. These venues also collect pooled financial resources. We can make progress in this area with objective investigation of our own pre-invasion spirituality. After hundreds of years, it is clear that the invader's religions confine us to oppression.

There is immense power in the rejection of the invader's concept of God.

There is obviously something wrong with his view of God. If there were not, he would not have invaded us. The most powerful non-violent defense is simply the recognition of truth. Equity is a by-product of truth. So the fight is for truth, not for equity. Equity without truth is unattainable. This is why the invader guides us in the direction of equity only. From a legal perspective, we call these efforts Civil Rights. We don't have to spend a lot of money and fight in court with the invader to reject his God and reconnect with our own creation story and beginnings.

Cleansing of toxic unverifiable religious dogma is a demonstration of love for God and self. Cleansed and strategic thinking will enable us to redirect the pooled resources of our people, particularly as it relates to organizing food production for the community. Our spiritual character will certainly be improved if we are not hungry and unable to feed our families. The military is the greater part of initial invasion, but the missionary is the greater part of maintaining invasion. In the process of healing, we find that the invasion cannot be maintained without religious dominance. Healing our spiritual infirmities is a process of investigating and embracing our pre-invasion connection to God. Liberation from religious bondage is priceless.

Our temples can also be used to redirect the education of our youth. Liberating education has to come from somewhere. Obviously, it cannot come from the schooling of the invader's State. We must develop and support independent institutions that bring liberating education to our youth. Specifically, we are referring to liberating ourselves from the twelve parts of the one, two three invasions. The first six from the beginning of this section are the military, missionary and corporation as well as invader taxes, overconsumption and predatory banking. The next three are mis-education and food control which lead to medical dependence. Clear summaries of the patterns and cycles of invasion and liberation will help heal our minds of the last three which are disorder, disorientation and distrust. Liberating education points in a direction of uncompromised self-rule rather than a direction of equality.

Equality is an integral part of a strategy of liberation. If it is not, then we don't have liberation. We only have a change of control at the top of a hierarchy. The practice of love for each other that underscores the central message of our religions is best demonstrated by a participatory democracy, not by a republic. Equity is a natural output of this type of organizational structure. It has become clearer in recent years that we have to increase our use of cooperatives, non-profits and mutual organizations in order to foster incentives that are liberating rather than dominating. Corporate America is obviously a cruelly dominating force. It is best to avoid categorizations of capitalism and socialism. This framework confines us within a box of the invader's economic views. The framework of a liberating context includes the economic liberation of indigenous people, oppressed people and is extended to the environment as well. For example, mutual banks can support local food cooperatives in the production of much of the local food supply. The incentive is mutual rather than profiteering. Fewer, or at least smaller, machines are necessary and less transportation is needed. Vegetable proteins are highlighted since this is a much more efficient use of land.

The economic question is whether or not we want to compete in the game for survival rather than competing on price and profit. As a demand of our human right to the survival of our children, we will have to control our own food supply and resources. If a foreign cancer is feeding our bodies, what are the chances of our cells surviving? It is well documented that the oppressor starves people into subhuman submission. We have a responsibility to our children to not let this happen. We should have learned from the so-called slavery period that we must always keep control of our land and food supply. Otherwise, our children will continue to be dominated by the slaver. Of course, this institution still exists today as many of our young landless males are locked away in private labor camps from efforts of trying to feed their families. Ideally, we could see the great wisdom in abandoning the cities in favor of smaller autonomous jurisdictions that we can control. We were separated from our land by the terrorism of the invader. A return to the southern lands would help to heal this wound. Without land, we have no future. We have to establish ways of defending ourselves and our land from the ruthless invader. Development and defense are part of the process of healing the open wounds of invasion.

The particular problem of health care can be solved by promoting and supporting more traditional schools of health care on independent and public campuses. The two pronged fight is obvious. The Civil Rights lawyers fight for our right to educate our youth rather than using our tax dollars to school the majority into consistent failure. Meanwhile we build our independent educational objectives with other pooled resources. Non-profit health insurance, for example can be used to help fund medical schools on black campuses. Our religious pools can be used to help with scholarships to the medical schools. There are many combinations of things that can be done. This is just one example. It is necessary, however, that we have the common goal of controlling our own food production and health care. With our own food production, we can prevent many of the current illnesses. With food security, we can cure many of the current issues with stress related illness. Plots of public land can be used for planting fruit trees and nut trees as we use our votes to gain control of public lands. Again we see how we can effectively work the Civil Rights side and the independent side of the problem together to solve the problem of liberation.

Liberation is here defined as a process of healing the wounds of invasion. This healing requires independence, meaning self control. This is not an abstract theory. This is the same way our bodies heal themselves on the inside. The body has to become free from the influence and control of foreign invasion. This process of healing reverses the damage inflicted by the twelve areas of invasion mentioned at the beginning of this epilogue. Becoming free from the influence and control of the invader, of course, requires solving the problem of radio and television programming. Trying to take over or compete with the invader's corporate media is unattainable. The simplest strategy can be taken from the movie, "The Matrix." In a word, unplug. Incredibly great power can be unleashed from this action alone. We have a spiritual and cultural responsibility to unplug. We need to have contests to see who can stay unplugged the longest. The discipline to avoid programming is directly related to freeing the mind. The mass-marketed mindset is heading for an inevitable clash with other people and the environment as we scramble for resources to further empower the self-destructive process of invasion.

Our audio and visual representations have to use alternative broadcasting approaches such as plays and the internet. Tyler Perry has shown us how well supported plays can be. This market would open dramatically if oppressed people would become unplugged. Starved for drama, we would go see something that we control rather than being lulled to sleep by the programming of the invader. The internet can be used, but it is not wise to become over-reliant on technology. The process of healing from foreign invasion requires a strategy for liberation and sustainability. It should be understood that we refer simultaneously to the sustainability of the liberation of the people and the environment from domination. One way of weaving the liberation strategy into the cultural fabric is to create a song like "Lift Every Voice and Sing" by James Weldon Johnson. In our case, we began by narrowing the twelve categories of invasion into six to share the acronym HERLEG as a foundation from which oppressed people can spring. We conclude with eight categories of liberation strategy to show how the chess game can be turned into a liberation game.

Chapter 19

A Nation Standing

A nation obviously needs ground to stand on. As a counterbalance, nations typically have spiritual ground that is cultivated just as carefully. As we overcome spiritual slavery, enlightenment can guide us through an improved understanding of our relationship with and in Nature. As with the Hebrews and Jews, our spirituality will enable us to finally unify. We have not been able to unify because we have not had a common basis for unity. Nature, as the central focus of our spirituality, provides an immutable basis for unity. This unity will enable us to effectively organize. Spiritual organization enables us to resist continuously. Resistance will encourage us to be more self-reliant, which will lay the groundwork for building our nation. Any nation must have a leg to stand on. Nations, as groups of people, are typically referred to using the feminine tense. Following this convention, we would like to offer an acronym of HER LEG to stand on.

An independent nation must control its Health, Education, Religion, Land, Economy and Government. In Part 3 of this book, we discussed liberation theology which fits the religious category in HERLEG. Each part is important and we have to develop them all simultaneously if we are going to survive as black people in America. Winning the game of life is about long term survival. For Black Americans, survival is about a careful and purposeful path to liberation and sustainability. Winning the game is not about social change. Changes in society are a natural by-product of emerging from spiritual darkness. Social change is not a cure for Black American issues. It only treats the symptoms of oppression. As we emerge from darkness, we can establish ourselves as legitimate human beings worthy of more than social change. We may find ourselves worthy of a cure. Health is represented by the first letter in our acronym and should further explain why a brief discussion of local food control was necessary.

Health does not begin with training medical doctors. Health begins with a human diet and human physical activity. It continues with seasonally grown natural foods and herbs. Most of Western European medical practices should be discarded in favor of techniques that healthfully consider the whole person. All of the European invader's pharmaceuticals should be avoided. These are drugs designed to rob elders of their hard earned wealth and to rob the children of their inheritance. The health of our local ecology has to also be an integral part of our treatment, or we will have recurring sicknesses indefinitely. We can start by teaching our children of all the foods, herbs and medicines in their environment before they start school and get boxed into dependent Eurocentric thinking. In order to become a healthy people, we will have to follow the aforementioned teaching of the immune system.

The first step was to recognize that which is foreign. We are eating a foreign diet of slave food. We are usually working/slaving for a company owned by foreign invading people. When we finish giving the best of our day to a foreign invader, we have no time and energy left to exercise. We are left mentally, physically and emotionally unhealthy. We know what many of our symptomatic health problems are, but we don't investigate the whole person or group enough to see the spiritual maladies underlying the physical problems. We cannot control our health without controlling our food supply including herbs and medicines. As long as we remain dependent on the slaver, we will not be able to solve our problems of chronic illness. Once we recognize the foreign nature of the illness and disease, then we can begin to neutralize its effect.

We can accomplish this by educating rather than schooling our children. This brings us to the second letter in our acronym, HERLEG, which stands for Education. Currently our children get indoctrinated with falsehoods rather than educated, which means to bring out who they are. The root word in educate, which is educe, means to bring out. What we do is put knowledge into our children's minds using the banking model that Paulo Friere wrote about in *Pedagogy of the Oppressed*. In the final analysis, our children get indoctrinated, not educated. It is inexcusable that we continue to allow this, even administer it to our own children.

How can we become free while we let the oppressor design a curriculum to program our children to emulate him? We cannot; nor can we become free while we design the same oppressive curriculum for our own children so that we can have a job working for the state. How many more generations of children are we going to sell out? We must demand from the state the human right to self-determine what we teach our children. What is the point of going to church on Sunday praying for the future of black children and then going to work Monday morning to mis-educate them? And then we seem surprised that the children don't want to come to school. Ultimately the poverty of our spirituality causes us to accept the uninformed and academically marginalized situation of our children. John Taylor Gatto wrote an interesting book on this subject entitled, *Dumbing Us Down*. This happens to U.S. students in general. Black students have a two-fold problem, dumbing us down and indoctrination.

Compulsory education is another way in which slavery is perpetuated. It is actually schooling pawned off as education. We need to teach our children to be able to recognize the difference so that we can neutralize the schooling effect of foreign invasion. In this section, we are moving from a broad heading of spiritual control through the biological warfare of the health invasion into academic malfeasance. From the beginning, the children's stories are destructive. In "Rock-a-by-baby" the baby falls out of the tree and is probably dead. In "Jack and Jill," Jack busts his head wide open at the bottom of the hill. Hansel and Gretel are about to be put in the oven. Incidentally, the Germans are guilty of putting people in ovens.

There are also more subtle stories that copy Eurocentric framework but change the characters to African. This does not make it a Black American story. We have to start by teaching our children stories that are relevant to who we are. There are very few of these available. Predominantly black schools should have not only predominantly black information, but also predominantly black teaching techniques. It should be obvious that this should include more music. Unfortunately, we have not been teaching our children to bring out who they are so that they can rule themselves. We have been teaching them how to be slaves, ruled by someone else. The oppressor teaches his children to rule. We teach ours to be ruled. The oppressor teaches his children to build a white power structure. We teach our children to fit into the white power structure. Then deeply mired in spiritual poverty, if we have fiat money, we think we are blessed by God. This is not spiritual, nor is it intelligent. We are selling our children's future (which is also our future) for a few extra dollars of loot from America's invader.

We have to control the content of our education, not just administer the state's oppressive school curriculum to our children. Taxpayers have to also hold administrators accountable for the content even though it is mandated by the state. For example, why are we still teaching Eurocentric history to our children? Some schools switch to African history as if that is going to do us any good. We still leave out the history right beneath our feet. The invader calls his story American history. As a result, American history disappears and is replaced by European invader history. Is it against the law for us to teach our children the truth? We need to know the history of Indigenous America if we are going to live in America. We don't need to know much about pyramids in Egypt. We need to know about the larger pyramids outside of East St. Louis and the older pyramids in Louisiana. It is partly our slave education that keeps us bound to looking for our identity in Northeast Africa. Another example of inadequate history is the civil rights history. We need to know the human rights struggles for liberation as opposed to the acceptable civil rights struggles for continued slavery, called integration. Consider that we learn of Rosa Parks not giving up her seat on the bus; but we never learn of Patterson Automobile Company, who manufactured buses up until World War II.

We learn of civil rights but never of self-reliance. In short, we have to demand a curriculum that reflects not only who we are, but also a strategy for survival. We have a human right to teach our children from a curriculum that is liberating and sustainable rather than accepting the same marginalizing curriculum that has been imposed to perpetuate slavery. We have to finally teach our children to overcome the tricks rather than to cope with the tricks. We can teach them to defend against the strategies of COINTELPRO. These are strategies that are used against them. It is imperative that we teach our children to defend against oppressive aggression. This is the only way we can stop them from pulling the same tricks on every generation.

Currently, we are not preparing our children to have a future outside of slavery. Our children must have a formal course in logic before finishing middle school so that we can communicate more effectively before many begin to drop out. We have to create textbooks that are designed for and by our view of the world. We have to create settings that work for us, which may not include a classroom at all. An educational focus on civil rights will not lead our children to freedom. Learning to think like good white people bound in black skin does not empower them. If Cuba can train medical doctors and educate her young, why can we not accomplish this with more than three times the population and many more resources? We cannot do it because we are still owned by the slaver. We are still connected spiritually, mentally and emotionally to the slaver. If we break the spiritual connection, we will be free to think on our own. We will make some mistakes, but we will sharpen our perspective and be able to build a future for our children. We can teach them local food growing technologies and solar power technologies as well as strategies to defend from oppressive aggression.

The problem of perpetual slavery keeps coming back to a problem of spiritual poverty. This brings us to the third letter in our acronym of HERLEG. It stands for Religion. We introduced six descriptions of God. These should help us at least develop a foundation of how to approach reclaiming our spiritual heritage from around the Atlantic, especially from the Southeastern U.S. The overwhelming majority of our people are from this area. So, we will use this part of the world and its influences to introduce some framework for our spirituality. Typically when black people take the introspective journey into knowledge of self, we also pick up on the 'harmony with Nature' vibe. As far as framework is concerned, choosing appropriate holidays can help us to align ourselves correctly. This involves replacing the disharmonious 12 month calendar and zodiac. We move through 13 moons (months) and 13 constellations (zodiac) annually. If we use 13 months of 28 days, then we will be back in touch with the annual cycle and the human menstrual cycle. We do not need to reinvent the wheel to accomplish this since the nearby Mayan calendar already provides framework for it. From this backdrop, we can create annual celebrations relevant to our healing and experiences.

For example, we would celebrate the Summer Solstice and Juneteenth as opposed to the Fourth of July. The Summer Solstice marks the time of year when the days begin to get shorter. We can reflect on the lessons from the periods of darkness and despair. We can put together a plan to ensure that slavery is finally ended and never happens again. A holiday around Juneteenth gives us an opportunity to tell our children the truth about 1865. It was the beginning of slavery, not the end, which evolved from us being prisoners of war. If we may digress briefly back to education, the Fredrick Douglas 4th of July speech is a good teaching tool for this holiday. The declaration of independence is also good framework for creating our own. We could discuss it thoroughly and expose to the international community how we have been treated 100 times worse and, therefore, have a human right to declare our independence.

Creating our own holidays helps us to neutralize the effect of the slaver narrating our experience. It helps us to remember to define and narrate our own experiences. It will encourage solidarity with each other. Our celebrations become part of our cultural memory. This is how we pass on to each generation what they need to know to protect themselves from invasion and dominance. Our children need to know that we love them and that we do not intend to allow them to be slaves forever. This is spiritual. Fitting into the slaver's devilish plans is not spiritual. The most important holiday trick is designed to empty our pockets and fill the oppressor's bank account. It claims a certain spiritual component, the birthday of Jesus. This is what makes it stick; and this is what makes it dangerous.

The practice of this celebration simultaneously perpetuates our spiritual and physical slavery. It is a great example of how we are taken away from what is really going on (truth) and led into a fiction story (belief). We see the damage of being caught up in a belief system. Every Christmas we give our money and thus our financial power to the oppressor, which gives them more power to oppress us. This is a spiritual trick from the Lords of Xibalba, the Lords of the Underworld. In reality December 25th has nothing to do with the birth of Jesus. We have found that the real reason for the season is the Winter Solstice, which occurs around December 21st in the northern hemisphere. The birth of the Sun is represented by the days starting to get longer, hence the nature of the Christmas birth story. Ancient people saw the days get longer around December 25th, but it was still a Winter Solstice celebration.

Fortunately, Dr. Karenga made an attempt to improve upon Christmas and its relevance to Black Americans. In spite of his great contribution, it remains inadequate for many of the same reasons already discussed about Afrocentrism in Part 2. We need to stand on his shoulders and keep progressing because Kwanzaa does not establish a relationship with the Winter Solstice. It, therefore, does not get us back in harmony with Nature. Once we get back on Mother Nature's team, we can be sure that we can win. We know that the pale man will not win in his battle against Nature. It behooves us to align ourselves with the winning team if we intend to have a future.

As the days get longer, the Winter Solstice marks a new beginning, a new Solar Year. The relevant tree for us during this new Solar Cycle is a Liberation tree rather than a Christmas tree. This is the newness that we must celebrate. Every year we look forward to the light of Liberation. The children can decorate the tree with their individual ornaments of freedom and then top it off with a household ornament or community ornament. We can do something every Winter Solstice to help liberate our children rather than locking them into a world of consumerism and trinkets. We will publish a separate document on holidays. We just wanted to expose how our holiday herding helps to perpetuate our slavery and introduce the idea of how to build some framework to house our spiritual redevelopment. The main thing to take away from the religious letter in our acronym is that Christianity and Islam are not liberating for Black Americans. Instead, we have to redevelop our Atlantic connection to God with a focus on the Westside since that is where we are. We have to teach our children to find spiritual truth in the cosmos, on the inside of themselves and beneath their feet. There is nothing we need to know about Middle Eastern religions except how to become liberated from them. The more we understand the relationships in Nature and in the cosmos, the more we will understand ourselves and God.

The next letter in HER LEG stands for land. We are terrestrial animals and we require land on which to survive. We have a human right to land and clean drinking water for our families. Government housing projects do not allow us to become fully human. Reservations do not allow us to become fully human. Integrated land does not allow us to become fully human. We are people of the Atlantic, predominantly from the West side; and we require a piece of the West side of the Atlantic to survive. If we are to receive reparations, then we must receive it in enough land on the Southeast Atlantic coast of the U.S. to build a nation for 40 million Black Americans. This is the only kind of reparations that makes any sense. We must get land that cannot be resold to the invader for any reason. With this land, we will be able to trade with other black people around the Atlantic without crossing any territory of America's invader. We must make them live up to the notion of free Black Americans. We realize the invader will not like this kind of reparations because he wants to be able to feed our children his story of Lincoln's proclamation as his offering of freedom.

More than a century later, we have to close the door on this false teaching completely. We have to explain to our children that we remain landless precisely because we were not freed in 1865. We are stuck in a political belief system about 1865 that is detrimental to our survival as a people. The invader's politics are foul. His religion is foul. His education is foul. We have to call time out and put together a plan to win. We need our lawyers to arrange for a sovereign state on the Southeast Coast. This would provide us with a place to be. Fighting for civil rights is inadequate and leaves us vulnerable to perpetual tricks from the dominant culture. So, let's be clear that Civil Rights may relieve some pain, but independence cures the illness.

We have to teach our children not to accept any more tricks of Xibalba. The sad fact is that we do not have any land. We are pawns in someone else's political domain. We do not have a black President because we do not have a country. We are subjects in an oppressor's country. The oppressor's political domain has a black President. We do not have strategic control of anything in the U.S. Most of us just do what is required of us by the slaver just like Obama. Otherwise, they would kill him. He is not the owner. He simply has the top job, which is not very credible considering some of the idiots who have been hired in the past. We have historical precedent in Africa and elsewhere of hand-picked black leaders of foreign invading systems. Things often get worse instead of better as oppression becomes legitimized by the black face.

It is our spiritual ineptitude that leaves us so vulnerable to the changing of faces. It is a trick from the Lords of Xibalba. If we get back to our spiritual heritage, the oppressor will not be able to pull these kinds of tricks on us. The top brass in the U.S. did not hire a black President until there was nothing left to Preside over. They have perpetrated so much terrorism around the world that they needed to hire Obama to help improve their image. Of course, they looted the treasury before turning over the reins to him. In this way, he would not be able to make any social changes that could benefit black people. To make matters worse, our new President took even more of our tax money and gave it to the so-called white power structure. As mentioned, this gives them even more power to oppress us. He has demonstrated who his loyalty is with. It is not with the masses of black people.

In terms of improving hunger and land uses, the Obama administration could organize local food growing as it was done during World War II. Of course, he will not do it because this would take control from large corporate farms and benefit poor people. What Obama is doing has been done many times over in Africa. He is perpetuating the system of dominance while blaming the victim. The dominant culture chose him to perpetuate their tricks as they have done many times over in Africa. Then after things get worse, they blame it on black leadership. What difference does it make what color the oppressor is? Freedom means coming out of an oppressive system, not joining the hierarchy of an oppressive system. Freedom is not achieved by changing the color or face of an oppressive system. Freedom comes with control of land.

There is a Mexican story called the *Popol Vuh* brings clarity to the changing of faces. But this is not an African spiritual story which is why we never learn anything about it and keep getting tricked by the same games on every generation. The *Popol Vuh* is from the Mayans and it illustrates the changing of faces from the Lords of Xibalba. We need to learn the story. At this point, we are just introducing it. America's invading Europeans claimed that religious freedom and political mistreatment gave them a right to political sovereignty. Obviously, our religious freedom has been denied much more so than the invader and we could write several volumes every year about our political mistreatment. As was achieved by Israel and the U.S., we must put an end to the abuse and declare our independence. We have a human right to sovereign land on which to survive. Without it, we have no future.

To contrast a couple of noteworthy men, Mohandas Gandhi took an ancestral spiritual path to independence. Martin Luther King Jr. took an imposed spiritual path to integration. We can learn from past struggles what works and what does not. We can be sure that there is no future in integrating with the world's destroyer. Integration has proven to be continued slavery. Integration is a trick from the lords of deception. For the victim, it is a gullible, slave-minded sickness. The chains have come off most of us, but we are still like pets owned by white corporations and municipalities. We can sit at the same dinner table or on the front of the bus, but we cannot be free. We can buy a house, but we cannot own the land as long as it remains the imminent domain of a foreign invading culture. They can put us out whenever they get ready. The entity that we pay taxes to is who owns the land. There are countless tricks played on us in this area.

In the urban areas, gentrification, redistricting, zoning, etc. are a few of the games played. Farm subsidization is another game played on black farmers so that we cannot feed ourselves or protect our seeds. Our federal tax dollars are used to destroy black farmers by subsidizing white farmers to the exclusion of blacks. This, of course, makes them effectively uncompetitive. As an alternative to continued landless slavery, liberation separates us from the invader's tricks and forces us into self-reliance with others of our group. It is similar to reintroducing zoo animals to the wild. It is also similar to the children of Israel separating from Egypt. These examples make it clear that integration is not liberation. We know that liberation requires land on which to live as a sovereign and self-reliant people.

It is from the land and water that all wealth is produced. This brings up the next letter in HERLEG, which stands for Economics. Currently, this is the science of economic domination. It is not simply a way of allocating resources. We know that we are being economically marginalized, meaning kept at the bottom. The Powernomics or Blackonomics strategy seems to ignore the history of black economic achievement within the so-called white power structure. In the early 1900s, we advanced rapidly and those economic advancements were taken away even more rapidly. Recall the Tulsa race riots which exemplify what was going on all over the country. As long as we are still slaves, any economic advancement of the people can be quickly taken away. The strategy used against us is to allow a few blacks the exploits of wealth, but to keep the masses grinding and hoping for something they will never attain. For example, the masses of hip hop hopefuls end up in jail trying to gain street credibility like the images we are shown in the media. Just as freedom cannot include being spiritually bound to the slaver, freedom also cannot include being economically bound to the slaver. In other words, if we are not economically free to develop and allocate our own resources, then we are not free. If we can ever become spiritually free, they will not be able to play all of these tricks on us continuously. Do we think God would have us economically bound to a foreign, invading, destructive culture forever?

We have to expand our thinking. Contrary to the Rich Dad, Poor Dad series, winning the game is not just a matter of winning the rate race and joining the landlord class. This remains oppressive. The individual gain never reaches the masses. The path to overcoming the rat race is to come out of the rat race altogether. The way to win this game is to not play the game. Western European economics is a devil's game of raping Mother Earth and her peoples. There is nothing spiritual about joining this game and trying to succeed in it. In fact, there is an alternative definition of success attributed arguably to Bessie Anderson Stanley or Ralph Waldo Emmerson that illustrates a different outlook:

> "To laugh often and much;
> To win the respect of intelligent people
> and the affection of children;
> To earn the appreciation of honest critics
> and endure the betrayal of false friends;
> To appreciate beauty,
> to find the best in others;
> To leave the world a bit better,
> whether by a healthy child,
> a garden patch or a redeemed social condition;
> To know even one life has breathed easier
> because you have lived.
> This is to have succeeded."[19]

If we are ever to succeed economically, we will have to make our progress outside of the slaver's oppressive economic paradigm. This is what history shows us from the destruction of black economic progress. We have to create our own economic rules on our own land. If we have land as a people, then we will have wealth. We can distribute our land and resources in a more equitable fashion. Equity was never intended to be a part of the current economic system that we have been subjected to. Recall that it was built on invasion, slavery and colonialism. Its design is deceptive. Where there is no equity, all that is left is domination. We are taught that the current economic system is the most efficient way to allocate resources. This is not consistent with reality. We are using up the world's resources to make an overwhelming number of trinkets and toys to consume that we do not want or need. This is not an efficient use of resources. The only reason we think we want these trinkets is because we have been schooled into a consumerism mentality and we watch advertisements that create wants within us. We used to build pyramids to God. As a result of so much inefficient consumerism, we now build pyramids of trash.

If we take a look at indigenous history, we will find that it was trinkets that helped to enslave us. So, we will have to not only come from under the economic ownership of the invader, but also break free from emotional attachment to his economic paradigm and trinkets. It is oppressive and unsustainable. Please see the following diagram that illustrates this reality:

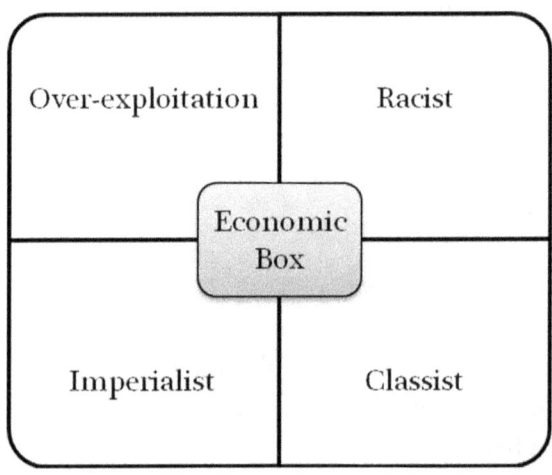

The economic box illustrated above is the capitalism side of the cultural box we illustrated in Part 1. It is also read clockwise. As we see in the top left of the diagram, Western European capitalism causes over-exploitation to an unsustainable level. Racism, classism and imperialism are also inherent parts of the system. All of it is destructive. We can start working our way out of this paradigm by taking over our celebrations and our local food supply. If we can feed our families, then we will not have to jump at the beck and call of the slaver. We can develop seeds for human nourishment rather than for corporate profits. It doesn't really matter whether we call it capitalism, socialism or communalism. The important thing is that our method is from our choice and is sustainable so that our children will be left with a legacy of survivability resulting from environmental responsibility. We have to start teaching our children to invest in each other. It makes no intelligent sense to invest in the same system that oppresses us. This is slave madness. We invest in the so-called white power structure through stocks and bonds, giving them even more power to oppress us. We are encouraged to help finance our own demise. By now, we should realize that there is no such thing as Black Enterprise in the U.S. What we have is black people reduced to the pale man's enterprise. The urgent problem of course, is that U.S. hegemony masked as U.S. enterprise is falling apart.

We need to make it clear to our children that Western European capitalism is not Black Enterprise. Then they can begin to develop Black Enterprise, which is more sustainable and equitable. We are terrestrial animals. If our economic plan is not land based, we don't really have an economic plan. We have an emulation plan, whether Eurocentric or Afrocentric. Imitation of the oppressor is not freedom, nor is it Black Enterprise. From an Indigenous perspective, an economic plan must be land based where every family has land on which to live. All humans have a human right to live. Since we must have land to live on, it follows that we have a human right to land on which to live. All economics comes from the land and water. A necessarily defensive economic strategy that makes sense for us begins with equal distribution of private land which cannot be sold back to the invader. There will only be a market for commercial land; but still not available to a previously invasive people or system.

This is simply the memory at work as in the immune system. It was step four of our explanation. (Recognize, Neutralize, Expel, Remember) We must have land that we control in order to become a healthy people. With political sovereignty and the land reforms described, there is no such thing as homeless people. There were no homeless and hungry people here before the Europeans came because the people lived in an equitable and sustainable human economy rather than in a fiat money belief system pawned off as an efficient economy.

The indigenous people of the Americas were some of the best allocators of resources in the world. Many of the world's largest cities were built here in near perfect harmony with Nature without the wheel, oil or compound interest. We should be studying the indigenous approach since we know that we are destroying ourselves in the current economic paradigm. Compound interest is one of the major problems with our current system. This is a well known game of usury and exploitation. Perhaps we can learn from Islamic banks about alternatives to interest. We can be sure that capitalism is not working well for any of the masses of black people around the globe. It is not just a 'catch up from slavery' issue. It is an issue of fundamental economic flaws. Black economists are not developing black economics any more than black real estate developers are building round houses. We have not succeeded when we have joined the exploiter's game of 'rape and destroy' for profit. We can be sure that the Western European model is destructive by a preponderance of social and ecological data. For this reason, it makes no sense for us to continue down the path of emulation while pretending that we are doing something black. Investing in the so-called white power structure is imitating the oppressor. It is not Black Enterprise. This is slave enterprise. There is no independent thinking involved here.

Towards broadening our view of wealth and success, we would like to offer another acronym spelled STEP. This encourages us to take a STEP in the right direction by creating a Sustainable Timeless Economic Paradigm from the teachings of our ancestors to the eco-friendly technologies of the future. Let's make the direction clear. Black economists, historians and other leaders need to get our heads out of the African sand and prepare a place for our children to survive in this land. Since most of us will remain here, we have to find out how Southeastern Native Americans were allocating resources and recreate this kind of efficiency and equity for the masses of black people in the U.S. If large healthy pyramid cities with ball teams could be built here without modern technology, then imagine what could be done today using solar and wind power. Tomorrow's economy will obviously have to be built almost without oil. In this return to sustainability, bicycles will simultaneously help us solve the obesity problem. We are suggesting that we teach our children to look backward and forward simultaneously in our economic decision making today. We have to start from a proven foundation of sustainability as demonstrated by the Indigenous culture. We cannot start with the Western European model and think that we are building wealth. This is boxed in support of rape, which ultimately destroys our wealth of resources. This is a lose, lose game. Studying the economics of happiness would make more sense.

A different view of the world enabled the indigenous people of the Southeastern U.S. to live more healthfully with their environment than we can now under the current economic and political regime. America had a sustainable culture of people living here when she became infected with a European virus. In less than 200 years of industrial revolution, the invading virus is taking the human family to the brink of extinction. We currently teach our children the more they act like the invading virus the better off they will be. This is obviously dysfunctional. It makes no logical sense for us to continue to learn the virus ways. Let's consider more healthy solutions. One way to make a positive change is to start working on the "G" in HER LEG. It stands for government. There is no problem with us deserving political sovereignty. The problem is that we do not believe we can achieve it. We do not believe we can achieve it because we have an identity crisis that confines us to slavery just like any other pet. We demonstrate with our behavior that we believe we are inferiors and the invader is superior to God. Looking back at our origins, the reason we search for God in the first place is that we seek to know who is in control of governing our existence. In the Americas, God is analogous to the center of our galaxy, the womb of heaven. It is in control because we revolve around it.

Our forebears looked to the cosmos and to Nature for longevity and ideal governance. Spirituality is always integrated with how we are governed. We looked for God through understanding how the real world works. This is what was written down and became the basis for our societal structure. A different story emerges from the Hebrew and European view of the world. It is based on morals that have more to do with dominant male rules rather than Nature's rules. The cosmic and natural underpinnings of the Bible are overshadowed by politics wrapped in religious clothing (Holy Scripture). We are left with little of spiritual value. We are left with dominant male ego governance. This is where we are today, locked into moralistic politics full of deception. Once people are detached from Nature and the real world, deception becomes an easy game for the dominant group to play. Unfortunately, this is a game of self-destruction for all of us. So, how do we stop the destruction of the world? We pull out of the destructive system which will reduce its power to destroy. As soon as we do that, the healing will start. Naturally, there will be a violent response from the world's most aggressive creature, the European invader. What we have to realize is that the longer we wait, the more people will die.

We do not have to secede from the union to accomplish independence because we were never included in the first place. We do not need a specific leader to demand that our people are released from perpetual servitude. Waiting on a savior is also a boxed in slave mentality. We do need a specific plan, like one that involves reparations of land on the Southeast coast on which to build a nation. If we are to ever have justice, we must have political sovereignty. This is clearly the only way we can begin to repair the damage of slavery. They can kill the leader, but with a solid plan, the movement cannot be stopped. We are like a many-headed dragon. We cannot follow a leader or individualism to long term success. We must follow a plan developed though dialogue.

Obviously, we have to account for the aggression of the invader to attempt to destroy the dialogue. But this does not make the task insurmountable. We seem to no longer be willing to sacrifice for our next generation. There are nearly 39 million black people in the U.S. Interestingly, we go all the way to South Africa where there are about 39 million black people to fight for their freedom and right to self-rule. Yet most of us have stopped fighting for our own freedom and self-rule since the 1960s. This is an outcome of having our experiences narrated for us. We are told that we achieved freedom even though we have no sovereign land. As a result of hundreds of years of terrorism, we are unwilling to see ourselves worthy of self-rule. We are like the battered wife who is afraid to leave the box. In an odd twist of logic, we see Africans as having a right to self-rule, but we do not desire the same outcome for ourselves.

It is time for a fundamental change, for a paradigm shift. Unfortunately, this change has been co-opted by the oppressor's game. In the co-opted scenario of change, things typically get worse instead of better. This time, they chose a black man to fool us with, to sloganize our freedom away. We ran to the polls as if we had no understanding of history at all and no clue of strategy and tactics. In the chess game, the Presidential piece is represented by the King. The object is to keep your King on the board working for you, not to hire your King to work for the opposing team that pretends to be integrated with you. There is nothing rational about this kind of behavior. We demonstrate self-destructive patterns like this over and over again because we are spiritually empty. Otherwise, we would realize that being confined to the slaver's political framework is a problem, not a solution. We have to build our political framework as we see fit. Black Americans have become disjointed, dysfunctional and disharmonious. We have been infected with a virus that causes great disease among us.

In the final analysis, we find that we must apply the healing BALM in various ways in order to cure the disease. The BALM is the Black American Liberation Movement. We cannot afford to let ourselves be tricked out of freedom again. After careful investigation and restoration of our identity, some useful framework emerges. We will summarize some of the framework developed in this book to help get us beyond the badges of slavery we carry around with us every day. It became clear in the 1930s through Carter G. Woodson that our schooling was a badge of slavery. It became clear in the 1950s through Elijah Muhammad that our names were a badge of slavery. Our desire to remain in the system, like a pet dependent on an owner, is a badge of slavery. Yet, all is not lost as the identity crisis is solved.

In contrast to the oppressor's ways, our education is family oriented to bring out who we are. The state oriented approach is designed for the needs of corporations and prisons. Our self-education will necessarily include some linguistic work as well. Clearly we have started to get our language back through the naming of our children. We have a long way to go. We wrote of the Muskogean linguistic family as our guide. Recall this is the language family of the Southeastern U.S. which is where most of us come from. As far as agriculture is concerned, we always planted in harmony with the rest of the environment with an understanding of balance. We had better yields and this is the most efficient way. The dominant culture lies to us in agricultural school in order to keep control of our food supply and thus our persons.

We have almost nothing in common with the invader except that we walk on two legs. Our economic heritage is communal and we have proven to be able to build on large scale with this arrangement. Capitalism is not the only way to build large scale projects or to motivate innovation. Our innovations followed the spirit of Mother Nature, not the spirit of greed. Our spirituality recognizes Mother Nature as divine rather than as an object to be exploited. Our architectural heritage shows that we naturally build round houses consistent with the round world. The oversized square houses we build now are badges of slavery. Better paying slavery for a big square house is what we have come to look forward to. Remember, a zoo animal with good accommodations is still in a zoo. He is still a slave. The solution discussed in this book is spiritual liberation which leads to political sovereignty. Our political heritage is that of a participatory democracy quite unlike the current aristocracy masking as a democracy. Just as our spirituality had no top dog, our political system had no top dog either. When the invader met with political leaders, it was a council at a minimum. Just as the Supreme Being is expressed as Unity in our spiritual view, our system of governance followed suit with a consensus requirement.

We have to start meeting on a regular basis. Turn off the television and go to a meeting. The agenda must be local to begin with. Whatever ills the community is dealing with can be discussed as we build our community farms and solar construction centers. We must come out of the food system that is killing us and come off of the invader's power grid. This kind of self-reliance is empowering. Stop letting the sold-out politicians come into the neighborhood selling programs that never solve the problem of slavery. We must hold our spiritual leaders accountable for the gospel of spiritual liberation. A few drops of liberation can flow into an ocean of independence as we realize the greatest form of worship is to live in harmony with Nature.

True spiritual liberation will take away our fears. We are afraid of the New Hampshire motto on the quarter that reads, "Live Free or Die." We teach our children to fight for civil rights instead of freedom because that is less agitating to the oppressor. In order to have a future for our children, we are going to have to express a desire for sovereignty and exercise our human right to self-rule. For those who want to follow the invader to self-destruction, go right ahead; but why not give your children a chance to build a future for themselves. We are not expecting to build a Utopia, but we do intend to build a self-determined place of our own. It is more intelligent to take our chances with Mother Nature than to continue to remain subjected to the whims of a foreign invading virus. It is better for the body to get the virus out. A liberation game and its strategies can help us do that.

Chapter 20

Liberation Game

THE offensive movement of the state persists in various forms. Historically, COINTELPRO is an example of an offensive political program. Unfortunately, these offensive programs encompass every area of our lives which makes it seem impossible to break free. The defensive movement has not kept pace with the aggression of the state. As a result, we are losing ground in every way very rapidly. Our progress can be measured by utilizing new chess pieces and teaching this to our children. A liberation movement must continue to be organized and energized in order for there to be some viable future for black children in the U.S. The never-ending offensive tactics of the establishment cannot go unchecked. Speeches and Civil Rights attorneys are necessary but not sufficient checks on state aggression. Psychological enslavement tactics must be met with an equal desire for liberation. The challenge is to expose the enslavement in such a way that it inspires a desire for liberation. It is dangerously irresponsible to wait until hunger and homelessness compel us to make a move on freedom. We have the 1960s struggles in hindsight to build on in the new Millennium.

In developing some fresh insight, we would like to explain an evolution of the pieces of the chess game. It may be a lot of fun for those who play chess. For those who do not, it is useful as a guide or barometer as to how we are doing in the struggle for freedom. It has been said that the European Diaspora thinks strategically while blacks think emotionally. This is, of course, insulting. Nevertheless, we can cure this situation with a specific, easy to understand strategy. The chess game provides this. We discussed analogies to chess throughout this text. At this point, we will summarize what Dr. William White taught about the original African pieces. We will then briefly discuss a liberating view of the territorial war game. We know the chess game as having the following pieces: Rook, Knight, Bishop, King and Queen with the first three used twice for a total of eight pieces. Dr. White taught that the original pieces were the following: an Elephant in place of the Rook, the Knight is still a horseman, a Ship in place of the Bishop, the King remains, the Battlefield Commander in place of the Queen. Like the contemporary game, the other side of the board repeats the Elephant, Knight and Ship. We can see some differences between the African mentality and the European mentality by the pieces on the chess board.

We see the strongholds at the end of the chess board represented by the Rook in Europe and the Elephant in Africa. The horseman, although unfamiliar in America, was common to Europe and Africa. There is a significant shift in mentality, however when the ship is changed to a Bishop. For example, the Egyptians did not use religion to dominate the Hebrews who kept their own religious views. Ships, however, were an important part of their rule. In contrast, Constantine did use religion to dominate his subjects and rivals. Thus we have the change from the ship to the bishop on the chess board. Kings are found in both cultures. The next significant change is to the Queen from the Battlefield Commander. It is our understanding that the reason this piece has such mobility is because it was originally the Battlefield Commander. We know that there have been African Queens in past wars, but this is not the typical case. European Queens do not go to war, but how many violent conflicts occur under the guise of protecting a so-called white woman? She is clearly used in the war game. As we build on this history, the new Liberation Game keeps eight pieces but none are doubled on the other side of the board.

The game relevant to Black Americans still recognizes the stronghold on the ends. Europeans used the Rook, Africans used the Elephant. For our survival, we have to concern ourselves with the Grocer and the Employer. These are the strongholds on our lives. As we grow our own food and develop our own technologies, we will be able to control our food supply and create employment thus getting these pieces on the board and in play for our survival of the game. So, the two Rooks or two Elephants become the Grocer and the Employer in the Liberation Game. One of the Knights remains a defensive player but the other was elegantly described by Gil Scott Heron as the military and the monetary. The Soldier/Ball Player piece remains on one side of our board, but the Keeper of the Pooled Resources carved out a space on the other side. It doesn't take a prophet to see the military and the monetary working together in the new Millennium just as they did to finance slavery in both directions across the Atlantic. The next piece is one we have already discussed, which is the Bishop. We need to get our religious piece on the board, meaning in the territorial game of life.

The invader has both his pieces of Catholicism and Protestantism. We try to use Christianity and Islam; but these are not our pieces. We discussed or religious piece in the section on Liberation Theology. Mother Nature's rules articulated through a Shaman will suffice as our religious/spiritual piece. Insight from this piece opens the magic of another dimension that can give us an edge in winning the game. The equivalent piece on the other side of the board is the Educator. This is somewhat of a religion and science parallel. Together, these two make up our belief systems. Often, we either believe in God because of religion, or we do not believe in God because of science. We have to get our ancestral spirituality and education back in play. Currently we worship an invaders God every week, if any. We also subject our children to destructive Eurocentric schooling. We have to get our pieces on the board if we want to be able to win. Using the Liberation Game as a barometer, we begin to get a clear picture of how we are doing in terms of preparing a future for our children. In most cases, we do not control our food supply or our employment. We do not control our spirituality, nor do we control our education. So far, we do not have any pieces on the board, so it is no mystery why we are losing the game of survival very badly. We are on a genocidal track with no future for our children.

With the aid of our diagrams and stories, we hope to have explained that we do not come from a hierarchal society with Kings and Queens. So, we know these cannot be a part of a liberation game. True to our identity, the political piece must be a Council as opposed to a King. The Council piece in the Liberation Game represents a group. The Council doesn't make decisions for the people. It makes decisions with us. It guides us to consensus. It provides us with the best logic and experience to choose from. It takes longer to make decisions this way, but why should we be in such a hurry? The Council piece is designed to further restore our identity and to heal our destructive hierarchal thinking. The final piece that replaces the European Queen and the African Battlefield Commander is the Healer. This piece has the necessary mobility to carry healing throughout the land. Of course, the board itself is a symbol of the land. It is a territorial game. The object of the Liberation Game is to get the oppressor's pieces off of our board, out of our lives so that we can determine our own destiny. This is the same way our immune system works to heal our bodies. Let's follow God's model of the immune system to heal ourselves and heal our world. Teaching our children the chess game with these new pieces can be a starting point for structured liberation thinking. The elusive quest for freedom becomes an identifiable goal of liberation. God bless our families. God bless us.

The following conclusion is a summary of the pieces of the chess game, the original African game and the proposed liberation game. Please contact us by e-mail at balmpublishing@yahoo.com if you are interested in playing this game online or would like to be involved with developing the graphics.

Of course, it is really not just a game. It is a strategy for survival. Thank you for reading to the end. We hope you have enjoyed our treatise on overcoming slavery. We further hope you found it thought provoking and action motivating.

Chess game	African game	Liberation game
Rook	Elephant	Grocer
Knight	Horseman	Military
Bishop	Ship	Shaman
King	King	Council
Queen	Battlefield Commander	Healer
Bishop	Ship	Educator
Knight	Horseman	Banker
Rook	Elephant	Employer

NOTES

1. Bullinger, E.W. *The Companion Bible*. Zondervan Bible Publishers. Grand Rapids. 1964. pg. 4
2. Carew, Jan. *Fulcrums of Change*. Africa World Press. New Jersey. 1988. pg.17
3. Posted at http://rwor.org in English and Spanish on Revolutionary Worker Online. Chicago, IL. #1245, July 4, 2004. (Speech excerpt from 1852)
4. http://historymatters.gmu.edu/d/5130/
   McKay, Claude. "If We Must Die," in *Harlem Shadows: The Poems of Claude McKay*. Harcourt, Brace and Co., New York. 1922
5. Marley, Bob. "Who the Cap Fit." Island Records, Inc. A Tuff Gong/Island Production. 1976
6. Aharone, Ezrah. *Pawned Sovereignty*. 1stBooks. 2003. pg.26
7. Aharone, Ezrah. *Pawned Sovereignty*. 1stBooks. 2003. pg.45
8. Carew, Jan. *Fulcrums of Change*. Africa World Press. New Jersey. 1988. pg.98
9. http://www.legallanguage.com/resources/poems/statuelibertypoem/
10. Marley, Bob. "Survival." Island Records, Inc. A Tuff Gong/Island Production. 1979
11. http://www.aavw.org/protest/homepage_ali.html "Muhammad Ali — The Measure of a Man." (Spring 1967). *Freedomways*, 7(2), 101-102
12. http://www.usconstitution.net/dream.html
13. Deloria, Vine. *Red Earth, White Lies: Native Americans and the Myth of Scientific Fact*. Fulcrum Publishing. 1997. pg. 40
14. Conlin, Joseph. *The American Past*. Harcourt Brace Jovanovich. San Diego. 1990. pg. 20
15. Wright, J. Leitch. *The Only Land They Knew*. The Free Press. New York. 1981. pg. 250

16. http://www.africawithin.com/clarke/concept_of_deity.htm
17. Deloria, Vine. *Red Earth, White Lies: Native Americans and the Myth of Scientific Fact.* Fulcrum Publishing. 1997. pps. 9,10
18. Rosengarten, Frank. *Urbane Revolutionary: C.L.R. James and the Struggle for a New Society.* University Press of Mississippi. 2008. pg.120
19. http://www.wisdomquotes.com/000158.html

References

Aharone, Ezrah. *Pawned Sovereignty*. 1stBooks. 2003
Bennett, Lerone. *Before the Mayflower*. Johnson Publishing. New York. 1961
Bockl, George. *God Beyond Religion*. DeVorss and Co. Marina Del Rey, Ca. 1988
Bradley, Michael. *The Iceman Inheritance*. Kayode Publications. New York 1978
Breitman, George. *Leon Trotsky on Black Nationalism and Self Determination*. Pathfinder Press. New York. 1967
Brotherston, Gordon. *Book of the Fourth World*. Cambridge University Press. New York. 1992
Budge, E.A. Wallis. *The Egyptian Book of the Dead*. Dover Publications. New York. 1967
Carew, Jan. *Fulcrums of Change*. Africa World Press. New Jersey. 1988
Churchill, Ward and Jim Vander Wall. *Agents of Repression*. South End Press. Boston. 1988
Conlin, Joseph. *The American Past*. Harcourt Brace Jovanovich. San Diego. 1990
Deloria, Vine. *God is Red*. Fulcrum Publishing. Golden, Colorado. 1994
Deloria, Vine. *Red Earth, White Lies*. Fulcrum Publishing. Golden, Colorado. 1997
Diop, Cheikh Anta. *The African Origin of Civilization*. Lawrence Hill Books. Chicago. 1974
Dobyns, Henry. *Their Number Become Thinned*. University of Tennessee Press. 1983
Easterly, William R. *The Elusive Quest for Growth: economists' adventures and misadventures in the tropics*. MIT Press. Cambridge. 2001

Eirera, Alan. "Elder Brothers Warning" Mystic Fire Video. New York. 1991

Forbes, Jack D. *Africans and Native Americans*. University of Illinois Press. Urbana and Chicago. 1993

Friere, Paulo. *Pedagogy of the Oppressed*. Continuum International. New York. 1970

Gatto, John Taylor. *Dumbing Us Down*. New Society Publishers. Philadelphia. 1992

Gatto, John Taylor. *The Underground History of American Education*. Oxford Village Press. New York. 2000

Genovese, Eugene. *From Rebellion to Revolution*. Louisiana State University Press. Baton Rouge. 1979

Gibson, Arrell M. *The Chickasaws*. University of Oklahoma Press. 1971

Hooks, Bell. *Killing Rage:Ending Racism*. H. Holt and Co. New York. 1995

Hudson, Charles. *The Southeastern Indians*. University of Tennessee Press. Knoxville. 1976

Jackson, John G. *Man, God and Civilization*. Lushena Books. Chicago. 2000

James, George. *Stolen Legacy*. Julian Richardson Associates. San Francisco. 1954

Kent, George. *The Political Economy of Hunger: the silent holocaust*. Praeger. New York. 1984

Kozol, Jonathan. *Savage Inequalities*. Crown Publishing. New York. 1991

Marcus, Bruce. *Maurice Bishop Speaks*. Pathfinder Press. New York. 1983

Marris, Sarah. "Curse of the Cocaine Mummies." Hilary Lawson and Maureen Lemire production. 1997

Men, Hunbatz. *Secrets of Mayan Science/Religion*. Bear and Company. Santa Fe. 1990

Muhammad, Elijah. *Message To The Black Man In America*. Secretarius MEMPS. Pheonix. 1965

Muller, Werner. *America: The New World or the Old?* Verlag Peter Lang. Frankfurt. 1989

Perkins, John. *Confessions of an Economic Hit Man.* Berrett-Koehler Publishers. San Fransisco. 2004

Pollan, Michael. *In Defense of Food.* Penguin Press. New York. 2008

Sheridan, Barrett. "The People's Pugilist." Newsweek.com. Apr. 22, 2008

Smiley, Tavis. *The Covenant.* Third World Press. Chicago. 2006

Steele, Ian K. *Warpaths.* Oxford University Press. New York. 1994

Tedlock, Dennis. *Popol Vuh.* Simon and Schuster. New York. 1985

Timreck, T.W. "The Mystery of the Lost Red Paint People." Northeast Archaeology Project. New York. 1991

Van Sertima, Ivan. *African Presence in Early America.* Transaction Publishers. New Brunswick. 1992

Van Sertima, Ivan. *They Came Before Columbus.* Random House, New York. 1976

Von Wuthenau, Alexander. *Unexpected Faces in Ancient America.* Crown Publishers. New York. 1975

Walton, George. *Fearless and Free: The Seminole Indian War, 1935-1942.* Bobbs-Merrill. New York. 1977

Waters, Frank. *Book of the Hopi.* Penguin Books. New York. 1963

Weatherford, Jack. *Indian Givers.* Ballantine Books. New York. 1988

Weatherford, Jack. *Native Roots.* Ballantine Books. New York. 1991

Woodson, Carter G. *The Mis-Education of the Negro.* Associated Publishers, Inc. Washington D.C. 1933

Wright, J. Leitch. *The Only Land They Knew.* The Free Press. New York. 1981